play & learn

Authors

Susan Elisabeth Davis and Nancy Wilson Hall

Consulting editors

Dr. Roni Cohen Leiderman and Dr. Wendy Masi

Illustrator

Christine Coirault

KEY PORTER BOOKS

contents

from birth & up — 1

three months & up — 84

six months & up — 167

nine months & up — 251

twelve months & up — 335

eighteen months & up — 419

twenty-four months & up — 502

thirty months & up — 587

three years & up — 670

four years & up — 780

five years & up — 891

foreword

Welcome to the world of child's play! Play is universal, and it's the natural way for parents to connect with newborns, toddlers, and preschoolers the world over. Playing with your child isn't just about fun and closeness; it's also one of the best ways to teach new skills, foster imagination, instill a desire to learn, and build self-esteem.

Your newborn will adore tummy tickles, peekaboo games, silly songs, and bubble blowing. In the toddler years, listen for more talking, singing, and laughter as your little one finds excitement in everyday moments. As preschool nears, your child will begin to tell elaborate stories, gain a sense of physical mastery, develop an amazing sense of humor, and still cuddle you close at the end of a delightfully busy day.

Many of the activities in *Play & Learn* originated from Gymboree's popular Play & Music programs. That means they've been tested by thousands of children across the world to ensure that they produce smiles, giggles—and learning. We are proud to offer this book as a road map for the fun-filled journey through these precious years. Let your imagination take flight: expand on our ideas, follow your child's lead, and create your own unique adventures together. As you nourish your little one's mind and enjoy special times together, you're enhancing your child's potential and building a lifetime of memories.

Dr. Roni Cohen Leiderman   Dr. Wendy Masi

0+
months

0+ from birth & up

milestones

Your newborn is absorbing information about her world every moment of her day.

- Her favorite entertainment: looking at your face. Soon she'll smile back at you.

- Her gaze is also focused on and tracking moving objects, such as a turning mobile.

- Relationships are key. A newborn views you as an extension of herself and loves to have you close at hand.

Newborns are engaged in their very first experiences with the world: their senses are developing, and they're highly attuned to you. Listen as your baby communicates by cooing, crying, and (soon) laughing. For now, play has more to do with trust, bonding, and comfort than with lively interaction. Playing with your baby can help develop her muscles and sensory abilities, too. Just take it slow, follow her lead, and give her breaks as needed.

1 soothe with heartbeats

Studies show that newborns are soothed by the sound of a human heartbeat, which they grew accustomed to hearing in the womb. Let your baby experience this comforting sound often by lying with him on your chest, skin to skin. Or sit in a chair and let his head rest against the left side of your chest, which psychologist Lee Salk and others have noted is the side on which most mothers intuitively hold their babies anyway. Notice how the sound and feel of your beating heart can calm your newborn.

2 look her in the eyes

Eye contact makes your baby feel attached and teaches her how to talk without words.

3 revel in his reflection

Babies are very aware of faces, especially those of other babies. Let your baby indulge in this fascination by gazing at himself in the mirror for a while. He won't know who's looking back at him until he is about 12 to 15 months old, but he's bound to like what he sees.

4 take cues from your baby

The watchful eyes of a young baby are truly enchanting, in part because they are such obvious signs of intelligent, responsive life. But young babies are only alert for a half hour or so at a time and easily become overstimulated when presented with too much activity. How can you tell if she's had enough? Make sure you tune into the cues your baby's giving you. She may turn her head away, start to cry, or become sleepy. Respecting her need for space or for interaction will give her a chance to control how much stimulation she's taking in. As a result, she'll feel confident about her place in, and effect on, the world.

5 lie under a tree

Together you and your newborn can watch the dance of light and shadow, feel the breeze upon your skin, and listen to the gentle *shhh shhh* of rustling leaves.

6 walk about

A walk in the great outdoors will quiet—and fascinate—most newborns, whether they're riding in a stroller or nestled close to your chest. Fresh air can do wonders for new parents, too.

7 tantalize with texture

Stroke large swatches of textured cloth like velvet, fake fur, corduroy, or satin across your baby's body. As his grasping ability develops, he'll start to hold the swatches himself and rub them between his fingers. (Make sure the swatches are at least 6 x 6 inches [15 x 15 cm], so they won't pose a choking hazard.) At around six months, he may even choose one to provide him comfort as he falls asleep at night.

8 satisfy by smiling

Smile at your baby often. This simple act makes her feel special and shows her she's loved. When she learns to smile back, you'll feel loved, too.

9 produce funny sounds

Your baby loves to hear you talk and laugh. You can help stimulate his auditory development—and get a good giggle going—by making all sorts of funny noises. Try squawking like a parrot, honking like a truck horn, or saying "hello, hello, hello!" in a squeaky voice. He'll be amused—and amazed—and someday will surprise you by initiating silly sounds himself.

10 dress alike

From the moment you bring your baby home, well-meaning observers will tell you how to dress your child. Often the recommendation will be to put more clothing on her. However, too much clothing can result in dangerous overheating. While newborns need to be kept warm because they can't regulate their own temperature, after the first month, a baby's body is able to conserve heat. Here's a good rule of thumb: for newborns, put on one more layer of clothing than what you're wearing. After the first month, your baby doesn't need to wear any more or less clothing than you do (unless you've built up a sweat from exercise or another activity).

11 flatter him

When your baby tries to imitate you, it shows that you're his first and most important teacher. So imagine how flattered he'll feel when you imitate his gentle coos, his sweet "ahhhhs," and his quirky, crooked smiles. It's a wonderful way to make him feel that he's someone special.

12 talk often

Your baby is keenly attuned to the sound of your voice and to your facial expressions—he needs to be exposed to both to learn how to talk. Speak gently to soothe him, or talk quickly in an upbeat tone and with a range of facial expressions to make his eyes widen and his little head bobble with excitement.

13 start cycling lessons

Moving your baby's legs in a cycling motion helps him develop awareness of his tiny body. It also strengthens his abdominal muscles and introduces him to the idea of alternating motion (one leg, then the other), which he'll need to master in order to crawl. You'll enjoy the face-to-face time that this activity allows, too.

14 play on a blanket

Put out a soft blanket and lay your baby on her tummy, so she can stretch out, lift her head, and wave her hands.

15 trace the tootsies

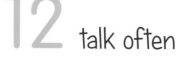

This light tickle game teaches about body parts.
Round and round the baby's feet
trace your fingers around your baby's feet
The birdie says, "Tweet, tweet, tweet!"
tap your fingers on her feet
Round and round the baby's head
trace your fingers around her head
Now the birdie says, "It's time for bed!"
kiss her forehead

16 listen to familiar tunes

Newborns perk up to music they heard in the womb—whether it was Bach, U2, or big sister's warbling rendition of "Rock-a-Bye Baby." Playing familiar music will stimulate your baby's mind and help her feel like her new world is safe and interesting.

 tip *Keep two or three of your baby's favorite CDs handy and play them to soothe her at fretful moments.*

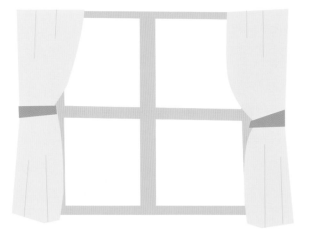

17 look out the window

Give your baby time to gaze out a window. The gentle sway of the curtains in the breeze, the flickering shadows, and the sights and sounds of passing birds will entrance her, as well as stimulate her vision and sharpen her ability to locate noises coming from different directions.

18 stretch out

Stretching your newborn's arms and legs helps your little one uncurl from a fetal position and become aware of his limbs. Gently pull his arms above his head, one at a time, and then slowly pull his legs down, one at a time, until they're almost straight. Be sure to stop if your baby isn't enjoying the stretches.

19 wear your wee one

You'll quickly realize that your baby's favorite place to be is right against your chest. Many babies, in fact, start fussing as soon as they are set down. Your infant's need for physical contact—and rhythmic motion—is natural; instinct tells her that she needs to be near someone to be safe. Satisfy her desire for contact by "wearing" her, in either a sling or a front carrier. An oft-cited study of mother-infant pairs found that six-week-old babies who were "worn" for at least three hours a day cried only half as much as those babies who were not. Carrying your infant also helps her develop the muscles required to sit, stand, and walk, because she is in a semi-upright or upright position, which naturally strengthens her neck and back muscles.

0+
months

20 dance to the beat

Dancing with babies is an age-old technique for helping them fall asleep or settle down. It provides them with the swaying motion and physical contact that they crave. Some babies enjoy lullabies; others prefer rock'n'roll. Whatever your baby's preference, swaying with him held in your arms is a great way to bond, and it does wonders to both calm a child and ease a stressed parent's soul. In years to come, hearing the music that you and your baby danced to will bring back tender memories.

21 pat her back

When your baby is fussy, sleepy, or just needing a little physical contact, pat her gently on her back. This action helps her expel gas, distracts her from too much stimulation in her environment, and simply reassures her that you're there.

22 dust the baby

Tickling your newborn with a clean feather duster helps him feel where his body begins and ends. Keep "dusting" your baby, and by about three months of age he's likely to giggle every time you pull out that "toy."

23 change diapers playfully

The chore of changing diapers can also be a playful ritual. Give your baby a clean diaper to hold, and take it back with a cheery "thank you." Then sing "up goes the bottom" and "on goes the diaper" as you change her. Just as a bedtime routine can help coax her to sleep, a well-honed diaper routine can encourage cooperation.

 tip *Set up a couple of diaper-changing places in your home so you can opt to use the one closest to you.*

24 smack your lips

Soft lip-smacking sounds soothe many jangled babies. The late anthropologist Ashley Montagu suggested in his book *Touching: The Human Significance of the Skin*, "The infant identifies the sounds and the lips from which they emerge with pleasurable experiences," such as being kissed.

25 play with paper plates

Use your baby's attraction to faces to help him learn how to track objects visually—that is, to move his eyes and head together to follow objects. Draw a simple smiling face on a paper plate or a round piece of paper. Holding the drawing 8 to 15 inches (20 to 38 cm) in front of his face, slowly move it from side to side.

26 listen to wind chimes

Hearing is the first sense that develops fully in a newborn (even fetuses can hear while in the womb). Wind chimes stimulate hearing (not to mention the sense of seeing), and your baby will love listening to the tinkling sounds while watching the dangling pieces sway in the breeze.

27 soar like an airplane

Hold your baby beneath her tummy with her face looking downward. For many infants, this position is particularly soothing when they're gassy or very tired. While supporting her head, gently move her up and down for a soothing and fun "plane" ride.

28 blow gently

Lightly blowing on your baby's skin heightens his sense of touch. Blow on his fingers, tummy, and toes while changing his diaper. It might provide a helpful distraction if he gets impatient during the process—and it might even inspire a smile.

29 make contact

Young babies thrive on the warmth of another human. One Swedish study showed that newborns who were given skin-to-skin contact with their mothers cried far less than those who were not. A recent South African report also found that babies given skin-to-skin contact stayed warmer and breathed easier than those who spent their first days in incubators. Even beyond the newborn stage, contact between baby and parent provides deep emotional and physical comfort.

30 blow on a pinwheel

The whirring movement and flashing colors of a pinwheel mesmerize even very young babies. To give your baby the best view of this spinning wonder, hold the pinwheel about 2 feet (60 cm) from his face and blow on it, making sure it's far enough away from him so that he can't grab it. Don't let him hold it, either, as the edges of a pinwheel could be sharp.

31 encourage daydreaming

With all the emphasis on actively engaging babies, keep in mind that they are sometimes content to simply daydream, just like grown-ups. If your baby is gazing at her mobile or practicing lifting and lowering her tiny hand, let her enjoy the quiet time. She's not only learning to entertain herself, she's also increasing her ability to concentrate.

32 blink your eyes

Stare directly at your baby and blink your eyes rapidly. It might just make him smile—and may give your little imitator something new to try.

33 read to your infant

While your newborn won't understand the stories you read to her, she will love being nestled in your arms and listening to the rise and fall of your voice. And studies show that because babies who are read to during infancy hear more words, they typically develop a larger vocabulary when they are older.

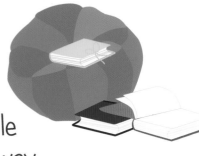

34 snuggle and sway

When your baby is unsettled, cradle him upright, chest-to-chest, to soothe him with enclosing full-body contact. Gently rock or sway while the baby looks out over your shoulder. Or snuggle him up under your chin, where he'll feel gentle vibrations as you talk or hum.

35 say her name often

Your newborn has no concept of who she is, or even that she's a separate being with her own name. Tell her her name often—and with tenderness in your voice. It will help her learn that she's both loved and unique.

 tip *Keep smiling at your baby. She will learn to "read" your face and reflect your good mood by smiling back.*

36 massage your newborn

The pressure and motion of a gentle massage help young babies' immature digestive and circulatory systems develop. At a time when you're relaxed and your baby is receptive, remove his clothes. Rub an unscented, natural, edible oil, like almond, grapeseed, or olive, between your hands. Gently touch and knead his arms, legs, back, and tummy. (Avoid products with mineral oil, which can leave a greasy film and block pores, and peanut oil, in case your baby is allergic.)

37 make silly faces

Since your baby was just hours old, she has imitated your facial expressions, learning to mirror your expressions and reflect them back at you. She loves gazing at your face, especially when you beam big smiles at her or open your eyes wide in surprise.

38 hold fingers

Your infant's grasp reflex makes him curl his tiny fingers around your finger when you stroke his palm. While this response is pure reflex, letting your baby hold your fingers promotes attachment and introduces him to the pleasure of touch.

39 follow the fish

Hold your child in front of a fish tank in a pet store, at an aquarium, or at home. Watching the fish dart this way and that will amuse her and help her learn to track objects with her eyes.

0+
months

40 smell the roses

Your baby was born with an extremely refined sense of smell. Immediately after birth, babies can even recognize the smell of their mothers. Indeed, one way newborns find their mother's nipple is through scent. Stimulate your infant's sense of smell by passing pleasantly scented objects, such as flowers, oranges, or vanilla extract, beneath her nose. She can't sniff voluntarily (that doesn't happen until about 18 months of age), but she'll enjoy smelling sweet scents in the air.

41 cruise in your car

Many fussy babies calm down and even fall asleep when they're driven around in a car. Sometimes that effect kicks in after five minutes; at other times it takes 15 minutes or more. See if your baby is soothed into slumber by a car ride—and have an audiobook or CD handy to keep yourself entertained along the way.

42 shake the rattles

Once your baby has demonstrated an ability to grasp things, he'll enjoy holding and shaking light rattles. His first rattle-shaking will be involuntary. But hearing the rattling sound will help him eventually learn that cause (moving the toy) creates effect (noise). Start with light plastic or cloth rattles; heavy rattles are too difficult for young babies to hold, and they can hit themselves in the head with them.

43 travel with toys

On some days, a tote bag full of goodies may be the one thing that will keep your baby (and you!) from having meltdowns in the car. Stock rattles, board books, and toys, and change the bag's contents often so you'll always have a new diversion readily at hand.

44 name that part

After a bath, teach your baby the names of body parts by gently running a soft terry-cloth towel all over her body, naming each stop on the tour.

45 dangle the ribbons

Indulge your baby's growing interest in color and movement. Tie several short ribbons about 6 inches (15 cm) long onto a bracelet or plastic clothes hanger. Flutter the ribbons in front of him, letting them tickle his arms and legs. As he grows older, he'll reach out to touch the captivating ribbons.

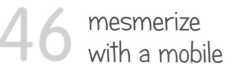

46 mesmerize with a mobile

By about two months of age, babies are intrigued by musical mobiles. With their swirling, colorful objects and soothing melodies, these toys stimulate both vision and hearing. Entertain your infant by hanging a mobile above her crib or changing table. To ensure that your baby never gets caught up in the mobile's strings, keep it at least an adult arm's length away. Be sure to remove it when your baby can push up on her hands and knees.

47 swing together

The peaceful swaying of a hammock relaxes babies and stimulates their vestibular system, the body's mechanism for maintaining balance and sensing movement through space. If your hammock is woven out of rope, cover it with a thick towel to make your baby's head and back more comfortable and to keep his hands and feet safely out of the webbing. Don't leave your baby alone or fall asleep with him in the hammock, however, because if he rolls into you he may not be able to lift his head to breathe.

0+
months

48 build bedtime routines

In the big, surprising world, babies love the security of rituals and repetition, especially when it's time to go to sleep. As you and your baby develop a bedtime routine, include activities that your baby finds absorbing but not too exciting. Practical preparations might include a warm, relaxing bath or spot-cleaning, followed by putting on fresh pajamas. It's never too early to start a bedtime reading habit, as a couple of short books can help lull a child to sleep. Then move on to soft music, a soothing lullaby, a feeding, or a comforting cuddle in the rocking chair. Consider starting a custom of talking about the day's events—the conversation won't be one-sided for long. Once your child settles into a routine, it can provide continuity at bedtime for years to come.

49 offer toys one at a time

As tempting as it is to give your child all of the toys, rattles, and playthings you've collected for him, hold yourself back. Since he can only hold one object at a time right now, having too much in his visual field may confuse or frustrate him. Give him one or two toys, and replace them when he appears bored. This will also help him focus—and prevent overstimulation.

50 tease the "piggies"

This traditional game will delight your child.
This little piggy went to market
gently tug a different toe with each line
This little piggy stayed home
This little piggy had roast beef
This little piggy had none
And this little piggy cried
"Whee, whee, whee!" all the way home.
tickle her tummy gently

51 play peekaboo

Look at your baby. Now look away. Look at him again, then look away. Sneak another peek—and look away. Now listen! He'll call you back with gurgles and coos.

52 rub those toes

Your baby loves to feel your reassuring and calming strokes on her skin. Gently massaging her toes increases her circulation and makes her aware of where her body begins and ends.

53 put it in black and white

Your newborn can see the high contrast of simple, large black-and-white patterns more easily than the subtle shades of brightly colored ones. To help stimulate his vision, hang black-and-white images—a mobile or framed fabric, for example—where he can see them. By about two months, he will be able to distinguish the subtle shades of gray almost as well as you can.

54 wow with shadows

Because babies are intrigued by moving objects as well as by light and dark patterns, shadows tend to fascinate them, too. In a darkened room, shine a flashlight on your baby's mobile or wiggle your fingers in front of a lamp to cast shadows on a wall. Watch as her eyes widen and she kicks her feet with glee.

55 sing with the spider

Although he won't be able to mimic your hand motions until he's about a year old, your baby will love listening to the travails of "The Itsy-Bitsy Spider." Add tactile stimulation by crawling the spider up his tummy, "pouring" the rain down his shoulders, and crossing his arms above his head to make the sun come out.
The itsy-bitsy spider went up the water spout,
"walk" your fingers up in the air
Down came the rain and washed the spider out.
wiggle your fingers downward to make rain
Out came the sun and dried up all the rain,
form a circle with your hands above your head
*And the itsy-bitsy spider went
up the spout again.*
"walk" your fingers up again

tip *Watch how your baby enjoys anticipating your gestures as he becomes familiar with a song.*

0+
months

56 dangle the toys

At around two months of age, your baby will start reaching for and batting at objects around her. Encourage her by holding a plush toy, a rattle, or plastic measuring spoons in front of her. Don't, however, hand an object to her too quickly or yank it out of her reach. To feel successful, she needs to aim for the toy and touch it.

57 kiss his tummy

Give your baby's tummy a tickling kiss. It makes him smile and teaches him where his tummy is.

58 mix things up

Babies lose interest when shown the same thing too often. So occasionally hang new pictures near the crib, introduce a new rattle, or find a plush toy that has a different squeak. Slightly changing your baby's environment once in a while will help heighten her awareness of her surroundings.

59 rock the night away

Never underestimate the calming properties of the time-honored rocking chair. Together, you and your baby can rock away the stresses of a stimulating day. Your baby will hear your voice, feel your warmth, and perhaps even drowse on your shoulder. He'll also begin to feel rhythm from the steady rocking of the chair, and understanding rhythm is essential to learning language.

60 do baby sit-ups

The infant version of this exercise will help strengthen your child's neck muscles. Simply lay her on her back on a blanket and sit at her feet, facing her. Then firmly grasp the top corners of the blanket with both hands so it fits securely around her head and upper body like a sling. Gently pull her toward you, then gently lower her. Slowly repeat several times—until she indicates she's tired by looking away or squirming.

61 pick the right moments

Babies are alert only for short periods of time. When your infant is calm and attuned to his surroundings, he'll be most likely to respond. Use these moments to introduce him to new toys, books, and music.

62 be part of the family

It's almost impossible to spend all of your waking hours interacting with your baby. But you can socialize with her while getting other things done by keeping her in a fairly well-trafficked area of your home. Safely tuck your baby in a stroller or bassinet and let her watch family members as they go about their business in the kitchen or living room. She can also hear them as they pass by, which will help her feel like she's part of the action.

63 get out and about

Beat cabin fever by taking short daily trips together. You can take your baby just about anywhere—to the market, a park, or the mall. New sights are stimulating and will introduce him to a variety of social situations.

64 bounce for fun

Add this jingle sung to the tune of "Mary Had a Little Lamb" to your knee ride for even more fun.
Oh, baby's on my knee, knee, knee
knee, knee, knee
knee, knee, knee
Baby's on my knee, knee, knee
And jiggling up and down.
bounce her lightly on your knee
Oh, baby's going whee, whee, whee
whee, whee, whee
whee, whee, whee
Baby's going whee, whee, whee
And now she's dipping down.
hold her to your chest and dip her slowly backward, while supporting her head

0+
months

65 stroke his hands

Help your baby become more aware of the way his hands open and close. When his fists are tightly clenched, stroke the back of each one, an action that generally makes a baby relax his grip.

66 soothe with song

She's too young to ask for a pony, but you can still please her with this melodic lullaby, "All the Pretty Little Horses."
Hush-a-bye, don't you cry,
go to sleepy, little baby.
When you wake, you'll have
all the pretty little horses.
Black and bay, dapple and gray,
coach and six little horses.
Hush-a-bye, don't you cry,
go to sleepy, little baby.

67 look sideways

At this age, your baby will tend to lie with his head to one side. Give him something to gaze at by placing colorful toys or simple drawings in the area where he looks. (If you use string to hang an item, make sure it's at least an adult arm's length away from the crib so it does not pose a strangulation hazard.)

68 admire sweet baby faces

British researchers recently found that babies, even newborns, are more attracted to designs that look like faces than any other designs. Babies examine faces with great care and as a result learn about the social cues inherent in various facial expressions. Show your baby the faces in this book and others. Which ones make her smile? Which ones puzzle her?

69 come when she calls

Responding to your baby's cries teaches her that she has some control over her world, that people love her, and that it's safe to trust those who care for her. Don't worry, you can't spoil a young baby. You can only assure her that her wants and needs matter.

70 greet him with joy

Your baby learns about a range of human emotions—including happiness, sadness, and the exhilaration of seeing a loved one—primarily from his family. Show him how people greet each other by giving him a big smile and a cheerful hello—and do it throughout the day. By watching you, he'll learn and soon imitate what you do.

71 practice patience

Newborns need time to figure out how to do what they want to do—whether it's reaching out to grasp something, kicking at a toy, or imitating your facial expressions. Be patient during these fertile moments. If you rush to help your baby or turn away before she's done what she's trying to do, she'll get discouraged.

72 balance baby

Gently roll your baby back and forth while holding him securely on top of a large beach ball, and he'll develop balance and stronger neck muscles.

73 change her perspective

Offer your infant a new view and strengthen her body at the same time by propping her on her side with rolled-up blankets or turning her over onto her tummy. Be attuned to signs that she's uninterested or tired—for example, if she fusses or cries. And remember, when it's time for her to sleep, lay her on her back.

74 shake a bracelet

Help your baby understand that he has his own hands and assist him in getting used to how they move by putting a colorful rattle-bracelet on his wrist. (Only use wrist rattles approved for infants.)

0+
months

75 create a baby journal

Maybe you feel you'll never forget her first fleeting smile or first bit of "ba-ba-ba" babbling. But today's memories will get crowded out by new events, as your baby keeps you in the present moment. So jot down a few notes each week documenting the wonders of early babyhood. Keep the journal convenient, perhaps at your bedside or in the diaper-bag.

Help your baby contribute some footprints or handprints, perhaps a series at three-month intervals. For clear footprints, ask another person to hold your baby while you direct her feet onto a nontoxic, washable stamp pad, found among scrapbooking supplies. Then gently press each wiggly foot to paper, gently rolling heel to toe. Someday, when your child sees these artworks, she won't believe she was ever that small (and you won't either).

76 hug for happiness

Numerous studies have shown that holding a baby releases the calming hormone oxytocin (also called the "cuddle hormone") in both parent and child. Hold him often: it will help calm you and your baby, as well as promote greater attachment.

77 give a mini-massage

If you don't have time to give your baby a full-fledged massage, just spend a few minutes lightly stroking her—from shoulder to wrist, thigh to foot, and chest to tummy. You may even find that your baby prefers this to deeper massage strokes.

78 dress with success

It can be difficult—and distressing—to dress an infant who's protesting: flopping his neck, flailing his arms, maybe even wailing. Try singing or playing peekaboo to distract him from the task at hand. If he doesn't like being naked, cover him with a light blanket. Choose easy-to-handle clothing, like tops with wide neckholes, pajamas with zippers, and pants with elastic waists.

 tip *Be sure to cut any scratchy labels out of your baby's clothes—his skin is very soft and sensitive.*

79 encourage head lifts

You are the best incentive to get your baby to practice lifting her head, which will help strengthen her neck muscles. When she's on her tummy, position yourself so that she'll see your face if she lifts her head. Call her name to entice her to look up. This exercise may frustrate some babies, so watch for any telltale signs of distress.

80 stick out your tongue

Babies are born knowing how to imitate many of the expressions they see on other faces. So try sticking out your tongue and see if your baby responds in kind. Or open your mouth wide and say "ahhhh" several times; he may open his mouth and say "ahhhh" right back.

81 set up a floor gym

Even if your infant is too young to swat at the dangling toys of a floor gym, you can still lay her beneath one so she can look up at it. She will want to touch the appealing colors and shapes so much that someday soon she'll lift an arm and start batting away.

82 bathe with baby

Taking a bath together is one of life's great pleasures—for baby and parent alike. Cradle your baby in your arms, play little splashing games, and experiment with textured cloths and sponges. The water should be warm but not hot. Before you get out of the tub, hand your baby to another grown-up or place him on a thick towel near the tub (never stand up with a wet, slippery baby in your hands).

83 make eye contact

Newborn babies can only focus on objects within 8 to 15 inches (20 to 38 cm) of their nose—the perfect distance for seeing a nursing mom's face. But your baby isn't able to track an object that moves from one side to the other. (In fact, she doesn't even know that moving her head along with her eyes expands her view.) To help strengthen her eye muscles so they can work together, slowly move brightly colored objects back and forth in front of her. By the time she's about three months old, these exercises will tempt her to reach out and grasp the object, a result of her budding eye-hand coordination skills.

3+
months

3+ three months & up

milestones

As your baby grows rapidly, he's also becoming more actively engaged in his world.

- Listen for babbling and take turns conversing back and forth with your baby.

- A gentle massage from you will help your baby gain awareness of his body.

- Placing toys close by encourages your baby to reach out, teaching him that he can have an effect on his world.

From three to six months is sometimes called the honeymoon period. It's a time of glorious smiles, belly laughs, exploring hands, and joyfully kicking feet. Many babies this age learn to sit, a core skill that allows them to see the world more clearly and to manipulate objects with greater precision. Infants are picking up social skills, too, such as babbling, giggling, and smiling—remember to keep up your end of the conversation and answer back!

84 sing loudly and softly

Introduce your baby to the notion of loud and soft volumes with the popular ditty "John Jacob Jingleheimer Schmidt." Sing this verse over and over, more quietly each time, until you're just moving your lips—except for the last line, which should always be sung with loud gusto.

John Jacob Jingleheimer Schmidt,
His name is my name, too.
Whenever we go out,
The people always shout,
"There goes John Jacob Jingleheimer Schmidt!"
Tah, dah, dah, dah, dah, dah, dah!

85 prop up your baby

Your baby's muscle control develops from top to bottom: first his neck strengthens; then his upper back, middle back, and lower back; and finally his hips and legs. But even before his muscles can support his body, his mind focuses on the idea of sitting. To help him get a start on sitting, prop him up with several large pillows. The cushioned support helps him develop balance and muscle strength, and keeps him from getting hurt if he falls over. As an added benefit, he also gets a different vantage point on the world: he's looking at life head-on, instead of from a prone position.

86 touch these

Babies learn through all their senses but particularly through touch and feel, often exploring with their mouth everything they can get their hands on, so place child-safe objects within reach.

87 marvel at the market

At about three months of age, your baby is the perfect companion for outings. While she still loves to be held close, she's becoming increasingly interested in the new sights and sounds around her. Whether you're at the store or the park, hold her and talk to her about what you see, gently introducing her to the larger world—colorful fruits and vegetables, children playing, or even the blue sky.

88 meet ms. spoon & mr. fork

If your baby is getting restless in a restaurant, introduce him to Mr. Fork and Ms. Spoon. Make the fork and spoon dance, talk, and pop out from behind the napkin dispenser or the menu (but don't let him hold the fork). Your baby will laugh—and you'll get good improvisation practice!

89 move up and down

To demonstrate the spatial meaning of up and down, say "up" when lifting your baby and say "down" when lowering him. Use a high-pitched voice on the way up and a lower-pitched tone on the way down, so he'll start to understand that voices go up and down, too.

90 enjoy an exercise class

Once your baby is more settled, it's easier to take better care of yourself. Many health clubs offer postnatal exercise classes that welcome precrawling infants as well. Aerobics or yoga can help new mothers get back in shape. While the parents exercise, the babies enjoy listening to music, watching movement, and receiving kisses, tickles, and smiles sent their way.

91 take time to listen

After the thrill of the first coos and babbles has gone, remember that your baby still needs to practice the art of conversation. To accomplish this, make sure she has opportunities to talk to a receptive audience. Give her time to untie her tongue and get some words out—even if it's just babbling.

92 whistle a tune

While talking is a long way off, your little one is tuning in to your familiar voice and starting to discern the everyday consonants and vowels that pass your lips. So surprise her by making eye contact and producing some unexpected sounds, such as briskly whistling or chirping.

93 enchant with a music box

He won't be dexterous enough to wind a music box on his own, but your baby will enjoy hearing its tinkling tune and watching the magical twirling figurine.

 tip *Play favorite lullabies to your baby at bedtime to calm him after a busy day and help him get to sleep.*

94 put on a water show

To help your baby develop fine motor skills and eye-hand coordination, give her plastic drinking and measuring cups to play with in the tub. Pour water into the cups so that she can enjoy the sight and sound of cascading water. (Never leave a baby alone in the tub.)

95 size him up

Ask your baby, "How big are you?" Then stretch his arms gently over his head and say, "Sooo big! Sooo big!" This promotes flexibility and body awareness—and promises to make him smile.

96 prepare to tap-dance

To help your baby get a sense of rhythm (as well as a better idea of what her magical feet can do), tap her toes along to the beat of a song. Soon she'll start tapping and kicking her feet on her own whenever she hears music she likes.

97 create a hand puppet

You have the makings of a puppet right at hand—actually, it is your hand. Curl your index finger into your thumb to form an O. Draw on eyes, then adopt a funny voice and move your fingers to make the face "talk." Your fascinated baby may even try to make his hand talk back!

98 roll her over

Your baby will learn to roll over at around five or six months. While this is a natural development, you can help her gain the strength, coordination, and confidence this move requires. To get her used to the motion, place her on her back on a blanket. Then gently lift one edge of the blanket so she starts to roll slowly over onto one side. After practicing this a few times, try rolling her in the opposite direction.

99 go bare

A newborn's skin may be too sensitive for this activity, but many three- to six-month-old babies love it: undress your child so he can delight in the feel of a warm breeze on his bare skin, a soft rug on his tummy, or the grass tickling his toes. As long as he's warm and not in direct sunlight, hanging out naked for a while is a great way for him to become aware of his body.

100 sneak up on her

Why young children love a friendly game of chase is one of life's great mysteries. Many relatively immobile babies also enjoy having you creep up on them—especially if you playfully announce, "I'm gonna get you!"

101 get bubbly

Shimmering soap bubbles, floating just beyond reach, are one of the many delights of childhood. They also serve a purpose: by watching bubbles, babies strengthen their ability to visually track and focus on objects. And by trying to touch them, they boost their eye-hand coordination.

102 swing and rock

This poem by Robert Louis Stevenson is a wonderful accompaniment to rocking your baby.
How do you like to go up in a swing
rock your baby gently in your arms
Up in the air so blue?
stop while holding her high on one side
Oh, I do think it the pleasantest thing
rock your baby back and forth again
Ever a child can do!
stop while holding her high on the other side

3+
months

103 imitate animals

Your baby is becoming aware of both the concept of language and the differences between animals. It's now the ideal time to introduce her to the language of animals: as you both read books, play with plush toys, or greet pets, make each animal's signature noise, be it meow, woof, moo, peep, or roar!

104 lift him up

Your baby's perspective on the world tends to be limited to the view from the floor, crib, and stroller. But there are many interesting things higher up, too. Carry him around and show him some sights: flowers blooming on a high-twining vine, pictures on the wall, or knickknacks on your shelves. Let him stroke the fabric of jackets hanging in the closet and the cool glass of a windowpane. Give him a chance to reach for snowflakes or the leaves on a tree branch. He'll get a big kick out of seeing—and experiencing—these discoveries.

105 click your tongue

Make loud clicking sounds with your tongue against the roof of your mouth. This may make your baby smile and even inspire her to try making the sounds herself.

106 play with ice cubes

Though your baby is too young to handle ice on her own, you can introduce the idea of cold by touching a wet ice cube, a cold cloth, or even a spot of cold water to her cheek or the back of her hand. If you're using ice, make sure that none of it gets into her mouth.

 tip *When playing with ice, let it melt a little first, so it's wet and slippery and won't stick to your baby's skin.*

107 give her a play-by-play

While many noises interest your baby, it's the sound of the human voice that intrigues her most. Fill her ears with language by explaining what you're doing, whether it's washing her hair, making dinner, or organizing your files. She'll be exposed to new words—and to more of your world.

108 bolster him

The muscles in your baby's neck are the first to develop strength in order to support your baby's head. To help the process along, put a rolled-up towel under his small arms to help strengthen his back and neck.

109 make mealtime a fun time

Babies eat while being held lovingly, and soon learn that meals aren't just about food. Feedings offer quiet times for eye contact and chats. Even before your baby starts eating solid foods, bring her to the family table, seated on a lap or in a highchair, and provide unbreakable bowls, cups, and utensils to wave and mouth, so she sees that dining is also a social event.

110 team up on chores

Babies learn by tagging along and observing daily tasks. Don't wait until your baby is asleep to finish folding a load of wash. Let him sit on the floor amid the clothes as you fold them, pausing to flap, shake, and discuss some items with your appreciative "laundry show" audience.

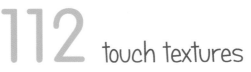

111 introduce the big kids

If you don't have other children in your household, visit friends with older kids or spend time at the playground observing the three- and four-year-olds. Your baby will love to see what bigger, stronger kids can do. Keep her on the sidelines, rather than in the center of the action, so she's not at risk of being accidentally knocked over in all the hubbub.

112 touch textures

Now that your baby is fascinated with tactile things, keep his tiny fingers busy with a book of textures. Look for animal-themed board books that feature fake fur. Or create a fun-to-feel book by gluing large swatches of coarse, silky, and furry fabric onto felt pages.

3+
months

113 bring a sock to life

For instant baby amusement, put your hand inside a sock and open and close its "mouth" while speaking in a funny voice. This impromptu puppet show makes a great diversion when you're changing your baby's clothes or even while waiting in a long line at the store.

3+ months

114 carry him like a flagpole

To help your baby strengthen his back and abdominal muscles, hold him facing away from you while you're standing. Put one hand just above his knees and the other hand securely under his chest. Now let him lean slightly away from your body—in a position that's similar to how a marcher carries a flagpole in a parade. Some babies enjoy being held in this angled position—so see if your child gets a chuckle from it, too.

115 put bells on baby's toes

Buy or make socks or ankle bracelets adorned with bells and rattles. These encourage your baby to kick to hear the pleasing noise. (Make sure anything sewn onto your baby's clothing is securely fastened so it can't come off and pose a choking hazard.)

116 introduce a new language

A child is never too young to hear a new language. One great way to start is by greeting your baby in the morning in both French and English with this classic song, "Frère Jacques."

Frère Jacques, Frère Jacques,
Dormez-vous, dormez-vous?
Sonnez les matines,
Sonnez les matines.
Ding, ding, dong.
Ding, ding, dong.
Are you sleeping, are you sleeping,
Brother John, Brother John?
Morning bells are ringing,
Morning bells are ringing.
Ding, ding, dong.
Ding, ding, dong.

117 practice yoga

In baby-yoga classes, your little one lies on her back or tummy, or in your arms, while you guide her body into adapted poses, sometimes with rhymes, songs, swaying, or gentle bouncing. Several books outline the basics, though you and your baby may enjoy the sociability of a class.

 tip *Some yoga studios offer mother-and-baby classes. Try one out to enjoy the benefits of yoga together.*

118 sing to the tune of a classic

Use your fingers to count stars in this song, to the tune of "Row, Row, Row Your Boat."
One, two, three big stars
count to three with your
fingers on one hand
Blinking in the sky!
open and close both of your hands
three times to make them "blink"
Twinkle, twinkle, twinkle, twinkle
continue "blinking" both hands while
raising them over your head
How'd they get so high?
hold out your hands, palms up,
as if you don't know the answer

119 double the noise

Soft squeaky toys instantly reward your baby's new grasping skills. Give him a toy for each hand. Can he hold onto both yet? Does he look at the toy that's making the louder noise?

120 sneeze loudly

Your infant is amazed by her body and, in particular, by the sounds she and others can make. You'll prompt a big laugh if you respond to her delicate baby sneezes with a loud, grown-up "aaaCHOOO!"

121 share family songs

Friends and family are often eager to help new parents but may not know how. So they might be delighted if you ask them to share some favorite songs and rhymes that they used to sing to their wee ones—maybe even versions in another language. If Grandma shares a few songs that her grandmother sang to her as a child or that an uncle hummed to you or your spouse, you're likely to develop a special connection to the song when you share it with your baby. And you can tell him its history someday (and maybe later he'll even sing it to his own offspring).

3+
months

122 whisper sweet rhymes

During your baby's bedtime routine, dim the lights, carry her to a window with a sky view, and murmur this traditional sleepy-time rhyme.
Come to the window,
My baby with me,
And look at the stars
That shine on the sea!
There are two little stars
That play hide-and-seek
With two little fish
Far down in the deep.
And two little frogs
Cry "Neap, neap, neap."
I see a dear baby
Who should be asleep.

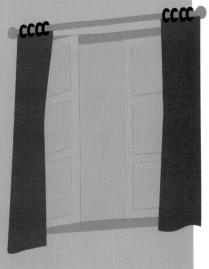

123 cheer on the bouncing baby

When your baby uses your hands to pull himself upright and starts bouncing, encourage him. Many babies can do this for long stretches of time, and that's fine—it's a great way for them to strengthen their leg muscles and boost self-esteem. (If you're holding his hands, there's also the benefit of giving your arms a good workout!)

124 give her a concert

Your baby's dual fascination with sound and with you means that she'll be a rapt audience as you play an instrument. Experiencing how music is created—not just hearing it on a tape, a CD, or the radio—will help cultivate her interest in music. Allow her to touch the instrument. Plucking guitar strings, banging a drum, or pressing the keys of a bugle teaches her about cause and effect and lets her feel involved. And when families play music together, children learn that music is an art form anyone can enjoy.

125 start swinging

Once your little one can sit up with a bit of support, he's ready to try a ride in a bucket-seat swing. Depending on his sitting skills, you can place him toward the rear of the seat or slump him forward over the front with a rolled blanket behind him for more support. Push him gently and not too high at first—his neck may not be able to handle racing forward and backward. If he enjoys the sensation of swinging, spice up his ride by tickling his leg or kissing his cheek each time he comes forward. Swinging helps develop the vestibular system, the body's mechanism for maintaining balance and monitoring its movements. These skills are crucial for learning to crawl, walk, run, ride a bike—just about any activity that entails movement.

126 make a ruckus

By three months of age, your baby is able to locate the source of nearby sounds. To help her develop this skill, move around the room while talking in funny voices or making a toy squeak or rattle. Praise her efforts as she looks, squirms, and even wriggles over to the spot where you're making all those interesting noises.

127 rock out

Infants enjoy listening to much more than so-called baby music. Downloading music online or listening to the radio in your car allows you to experiment with a variety of musical styles to find out what your child likes most. Encourage your budding music critic to kick and wave her arms whenever you turn on the tunes.

128 ask questions

Engage your baby by asking her questions. These can be the pleasantries of small talk: "How are you?" or "Isn't it a lovely day?" Or they can be more specific: "Are you warm in that jacket?" Wait for your baby to answer even if her response is just a string of babbled sounds. This teaches her the rhythm of conversation. In a few years, she'll be the one asking the questions!

129 giggle together

Show your infant that he's special and that his joy delights you—and how laughter, like all good things, is best when shared. When he giggles, giggle with him.

130 roll for the toy

Tempt your baby to reach out and grasp things by placing a toy just off to the side of where she's lying. As she gets older, place the toy a bit farther away, which will inspire her to roll over to reach it.

3+ months

131 appreciate books anew

You want your baby to look at the pictures and enjoy the cute story in her new board book, but she has other ideas: she pops the book right into her mouth. Don't worry—children's board and cloth books are made to withstand some baby gumming action. And at this stage, your child will explore much of her environment by putting things in her mouth. So let her gum books to her heart's delight. Eventually she'll explore them with her hands, eyes, and mind, too!

132 react to his cough

At about five months of age, lots of babies make an exciting discovery: they learn how to cough on purpose to get the attention of grown-ups. Once you're sure your little actor is coughing for effect and not because he's ill or choking, play along with his antics. Try imitating him after he gives a little cough, or putting your hands on your cheeks in wide-eyed surprise. He'll repeat his action often to prompt your humorous responses.

133 play with fabric

Babies and young children love experimenting with fabrics—whether it's a soft blanket or a colorful scarf billowing overhead. A tactile version of peekaboo combines this fascination with an ever-popular game. Drape a receiving blanket, a scarf, or a lightweight cloth over your little one's head, then whisk it off again—sometimes quickly, sometimes slowly. When she apears, greet her with a cheery "Hello!" or "Peekaboo!"

134 kiss the toes

Your baby will giggle with delight if you recite this ditty while kissing his toes.
One, two, three, four, five
Hey, baby! These toes are alive!

135 rhyme in the rain

Try this easy chant while holding your baby in your arms at a window or out in a light rain:
Water, water everywhere
turn your head to look around
Water, water in your hair
pat the top of your baby's head
Water, water on the ground
look down at the ground
Water, water all around
turn gently in a circle

136 give her target practice

Help your baby strengthen her leg muscles, develop eye-foot coordination, and just have fun by letting her kick at objects you hold near her feet. Use soft balls, plush toys, or whatever catches her eye and tempts her feet. For an added bonus, choose objects that make noise when struck, so your baby learns about cause and effect.

137 vary the carrying

Car seats that can be moved from car to stroller to house, while convenient, don't offer a baby much physical stimulation. All infants need to be held. In your arms is a great way for them to travel when you're walking, as those arms are the safest and most interesting place to be. After all, caring touch is a powerful form of communication.

3+ months

138 sing to amuse him

Sing the endearing peekaboo song "Where Is Baby?" to the tune of "Frère Jacques."
Where is baby?
Where is baby?
cup hands around your eyes as if searching
Where can he be?
Where can he be?
pretend to scan the horizon, searching
Where's my silly baby?
Where's my silly baby?
shrug your shoulders and put your hands out, palms up
Ding dong dee!
Ding dong dee!
"find" your baby and give him a kiss

 tip *Make big, bold gestures to accompany your singing—your baby will love the drama!*

139 create light shows

Help your baby strengthen his focus and visual tracking abilities by shining a flashlight on the wall in a darkened room. Try moving the light up onto the ceiling, then down the wall, creeping closer to him. He may try to reach out and touch the light!

140 crush some chips

Stuck in line at the supermarket? Hand your baby a sealed bag of potato chips to crinkle and crush (but not to eat). She'll be diverted for at least a little while by the sound and texture of her new "toy"—a small price to pay to avoid a potential meltdown.

141 make mobiles

Even though your baby's ability to focus on things in the distance is improving, he'll often prefer to look at details nearby. To provide a choice, securely attach colorful, lightweight objects to the stroller cover so they dangle just out of his reach. Keep them on top of the cover while he enjoys the scenery, and flip them down into view when he gets restless.

142 let her get mouthy

Allow your baby to suck on your sleeve, gum her soft blocks, and stick her big, noisy rattle in her mouth. Once you get beyond the drool factor and the fear of germs, you'll see that her mouth is one of her primary tools of exploration. So let her use it to learn about the world—just make sure that nothing sharp, toxic, or small enough to swallow is within reach.

143 tickle, tickle

Tickle your baby gently at every opportunity. His favorite part will probably be guessing where you'll tickle next: fingers, toes, belly, or nose?

144 get ready to go

Your infant might be wriggling across the floor or rocking back and forth on her hands and knees with a clear desire to get moving. Help her get the front of her body and the back end working together by placing desirable objects, such as favorite toys, just out of her reach. This encourages her to be aware of objects as well as her own body, and tests out her precrawling skills. Soon her urge to grab the objects will overcome her confusion about the mechanics of how to get there—and she'll succeed!

145 turn up the volume

As your baby begins to babble, he'll also start experimenting with the volume of his voice. Without startling him, show him how your own voice can get louder—as well as quieter. He may follow right along.

146 teach her to sit

It takes some time for babies to learn how to balance on their bottoms well enough to sit. You can help your infant gain stability by putting her legs in a diamond-shaped position. Move her heels closer to her bottom, bending her knees out to the sides. With a wider base, she's less likely to topple.

147 mimic each other

Your baby has shown you that he can stick out his tongue and smile to copy your expressions. He may even be imitating some of your sounds (like "ma-ma" and "ba-ba"). Introduce a new mimicking game by showing him how to open his mouth wide or how to blow raspberries, then watch to see if he'll join in.

148 boogie to the music

Gently support your baby and dance with her to lively music. Have someone stop the music and yell, "Freeze!" Stop dancing—and see how she reacts to the sudden change. When the music starts again, resume dancing. Repeat the same sequence. Soon she'll giggle each time you stop.

149 fashion a toy-blanket

Toy-blankets enliven tummy-time and encourage reaching and scooting. You can make your own by sewing together large squares of colorful, assorted, very tactile fabrics—velvet, corduroy, fleece, vinyl, satin, or canvas. (Make sure the pieces are washable, and prewash them before assembling.) Sew the patchwork onto a heavy piece of cloth as a backing. Stitch on loops to firmly secure rattles, the back covers of cloth books, and teething rings. Then let your baby explore this easily portable play area.

150 have fun with fingerplay

Add hand gestures to the song "Yankee Doodle" to make it even more fun for your little one.
Yankee Doodle went to town,
"walk" the fingers of one of your hands across the palm of the other
A-riding on a pony,
pretend to hold onto the reins of a bridle
Stuck a feather in his cap
mime sticking a feather in a hat
And called it "macaroni."
whirl your index finger around in a circle

151 explore a garden

While babies can't tell the difference between tulips and ferns, they recognize a beautiful place when they see it. Spend time with your baby in gardens or parks; she'll be enchanted by the waving branches, colorful blooms, singing birds, and wonderful smells.

152 repeat sounds

Your babbling baby enjoys repeating sounds. But he might be surprised to hear you do the same. Try repeating, with gusto, a single, fairly silly word (like "banana") for a startled reaction or maybe a belly laugh from your little linguist.

153 prepare her to crawl

Position your baby on her tummy for this precrawling exercise. Gently place the palms of your hands under her feet. She'll learn to push her feet against your hands, which will thrust her forward—ever so slightly at first. As she gets used to the exercise, she'll cover more ground with each push and get a clearer idea of how this crawling business actually works.

154 tickle her fancy

Try another little rhyme with a ticklish finish.
Round and round the garden,
with my teddy bear
circle your baby's belly
with your index finger
One step, two step—tickle
her under there!
"walk" your fingers up and
tickle under her chin

155 seek special recognition

Naturally you long to hear your baby
say your name. So when he babbles
"ma-ma" or "da-da," respond with
a smile and say "Here's Mommy!"
or "Here's Daddy!" He'll see that
some sounds net big responses.

156 describe everything

Start to encourage your baby's
observation skills by giving her a
detailed running commentary on
everything you see—from your red
hat to a large black cat—even if she
doesn't yet know what colors are.

157 talk about body parts

By frequently repeating the names of body
parts to your baby, you'll help her learn what
her body does and build her receptive vocabulary
(the number of words she understands). Try
to use body-part names in the course of everyday speech, rather than in a dull recitation.
For example, instead of saying "These are
your toes, and these are your hands," try
something like "Let's get these little toes into
your socks" or "Are your hands sticky?"—and
emphasize the word you are teaching her. This
builds her vocabulary and introduces more
complex sentence structures.

3+
months

158 swing around the clock

Your baby will enjoy swinging from side to side like the pendulum of a cuckoo clock, even if she won't be able to tell time for years to come.
Tick tock, tick tock
hold your baby securely under her arms and gently swing her from side to side
I'm a little cuckoo clock.
continue swinging
Tick tock, tick tock
continue swinging
Now I'm striking one o'clock.
lift your baby above your head one time
Cuckoo! Cuckoo!
swing her from side to side; repeat by adding two o'clock and three o'clock, and lifting up your baby two and three times, respectively

3+ months

159 play footsie

Combine gentle tickles with this playful rhyme.
Shoe a little horse
pat the bottom of your baby's right foot
Shoe a little mare
pat the bottom of your baby's left foot
But let the little coltie go bare, bare, bare!
tickle the bottoms of both feet

160 toss a beach ball

Enchant your baby with the motion and color of a gently tossed inflatable beach ball. Lay him on his back, then throw the ball in the air and catch it above him—again and again. He'll love watching it sail through the air—and he'll enjoy the surprise of seeing you catch it just before it reaches him.

161 saddle up for a knee ride

Sit your baby facing toward you on your knees, and hold her securely around her middle as you treat her to a lively—but gentle—knee ride. As she rides, vary your tempo, pitch, and volume.
The farmer's horse goes ho-dee-ho, ho-dee-ho
gently sway your baby forward and backward, as if she were on a very fat, waddling horse
The lady's horse goes trip-trop, trip-trop
alternate bouncing each knee slowly up and down
The gentleman's horse goes trot-trot, trot-trot
simultaneously bounce both knees quickly up and down
But (say your baby's name) horse goes gallopy, gallopy, gallopy, gallopy!
alternate bouncing each knee quickly up and down

 tip *Always make sure you are supporting your baby's head and neck when you are bouncing him.*

162 revel in quiet time

Babies are loads of fun at this stage: curious, sociable, and unbelievably cute. They love to interact, but need breaks from social stimulation, too. Don't interrupt your baby if you see her fiddling with carpet fibers, staring out the window, or playing with her toes. Sometimes she just needs time to explore the world in a quiet way.

163 trot like a pony

Hold your baby securely on one knee. Gently raise it up and down as you chant this English nursery rhyme.
Ride a cockhorse to Banbury Cross
To see a fine lady upon her white horse.
With rings on her fingers and bells on her toes,
She shall hear music wherever she goes.

164 pop a bubble

Elicit glee and giggles by blowing a big chewing-gum bubble for your baby. Then—snap!—pop it back into your mouth.

165 hop like popcorn

Your baby will smile at this sprightly fingerplay, even though he's too young to eat popcorn.
I woke up this morning
stretch your arms above your head, as if waking
And what did I see?
frame your eyes with your hands as if looking through binoculars
Popcorn popping on my apple tree!
quickly raise and lower your arms several times while opening and shutting your hands (like popping corn)
Spring has brought me a big surprise
continue to raise and lower your arms while opening and shutting your hands
Popcorn popping right before my eyes!
continue opening and shutting your hands

166 bounce or balance

It may seem impossible for a baby to develop a sense of balance when she has just two main positions: lying down and sitting. The key is making sure she has plenty of opportunities to move around, too. Spinning, rocking, and bouncing all develop the vestibular system in the inner ear, which is responsible for a sense of balance and an awareness of where the body is in space. To gently stimulate that part of your baby's ears, put her on a bed (lying down, sitting, or "standing" with support) and very gently bounce the mattress.

6+ six months & up

6+
months

milestones

Your baby delights increasingly in playing with you and capturing your attention.

• Watch him explore more independently as he starts to creep, crawl, and pull himself up.

• Read, sing, and clap together to build the foundation for language and communication skills.

• The forefinger and thumb pincer movement is a fine-motor developmental milestone that allows him to pick up small objects.

Your six-month-old is charmingly social, laughing and calling out to win your attention. He's also rolling over and beginning to move around to get what he wants. He will test his emerging fine motor skills by fiddling with his toys or food. And he's starting to understand that objects exist even when they aren't visible: a conceptual milestone that lets him be an active participant—rather than a spectator—in hiding games like peekaboo.

167 enjoy a rainy-day walk

Grandma may scold; a neighbor may shake his head. But letting your baby feel a little rain on a mild day is perfectly safe, perfectly legal, and perfectly delightful. It stimulates her senses of touch, smell, and taste, and can promote bonding as you and your baby explore the wet world beyond your front door. Make sure her rain gear keeps her warm and dry—only her face and hands should be peeping out!

168 stand up

Now that your baby's leg muscles are getting stronger, he can stand with your aid. Lay him on his back with his feet facing you, then gently help him rise to a sitting and then a standing position.

169 play tug-of-war

Give your infant one end of a cloth diaper or blanket to hold, then pull gently on the other end. As she pulls, increase your resistance a tiny bit. This gentle tugging game helps her develop upper-body strength and a sense of success. (Just don't pull so hard that she'll tumble backward if she lets go!)

170 go barefoot

Going barefoot is the best way for an infant to learn how his little feet work. It also makes it easier for him to figure out how to rock back and forth to find the "sweet spot" that gives him balance, because he'll be able to feel the subtle contractions of the muscles that keep him upright. Slip nonskid socks on cold feet, and put shoes on if he's treading anyplace where sharp objects might be present. But if he's indoors or outdoors on a safe surface, he'll be fine going barefoot.

171 follow the falling leaves

Watching the twirling motion of falling leaves and hearing them crunch as the two of you step or roll on them will fascinate your baby. Let her try to catch the leaves as they fall—even if she never actually captures them, she will hone her eye-hand coordination.

172 track the toy

While your baby can now track objects passing back and forth before his eyes, it's not until about his seventh month that he'll be able to follow items moving up and down. Move a toy slowly up and down about 10 inches (25 cm) in front of him. See if he can follow it; if he can't, try again in a few weeks.

173 blow water bubbles

Using a straw, blow bubbles in a glass of water. The turbulent motion will catch your baby's attention, and the gurgling sounds will intrigue her. Don't let her try this trick herself, though, just let her enjoy watching you and listening to the sound.

174 jump to it

This game gives your baby a perfect blend of reassuring repetitions with a dash of surprise. Hold him braced against your chest, slowly chant "One, two, three, jump!" and finish with a sudden hop. Repeat, but vary the tempo, speeding up the counting or slowing it down to create suspense leading up to the final hop.

175 create a rainbow

Show your baby how a prism can turn sunlight into a shimmering rainbow. Hang the prism in front of a bright window, or hold it in your hand and make the light dance around the room. Or try adjusting a glass of water on a sunny windowsill until it creates a rainbow (which she might try to grab) on the floor.

176 experiment with sound

If your little percussionist enjoys banging on pots, treat him to a new sound by swirling a cup or two of water in a metal mixing bowl while one of you strikes it with a metal spoon. The moving water extends the bang into a wavering tone worthy of science fiction.

177 ring the doorbell

As your baby turns into a reckless explorer, keep quick, easy amusements on tap, such as the doorbell-distraction game. Simply scoop her up, go to the front door, and demonstrate the magic of the doorbell. Show your baby how she can press the button herself—she'll be wowed at how she can fill the place with sound.

 tip *Make a "baby sleeping" sign and hang it near your doorbell to prevent unwanted disturbances.*

178 rattle a rain stick

When turned upside down, this South American musical instrument—a long tube filled with beads, dried beans, or pebbles—sounds like a rain shower; when shaken, it makes an intriguing rattle. Playing with a child-size version helps your little rainmaker develop fine motor skills and teaches her about cause and effect.

179 explore the looking glass

Hold your baby in your arms as you stand in front of a mirror and ask, "Who's that?" Talk about who you see there: "Is that Baby? Is that Mommy?" Seeing your smiling face may make him smile, too.

180 blow a kiss

It may take a year or two before your beloved baby can master the art of blowing a kiss. But when you blow a kiss to her, she'll understand that you're sending affection her way—and she may even enjoy trying to emulate your actions.

181 introduce activity books

Now that your baby's fine motor skills are more developed, he'll love opening the flaps, pushing the buttons, and stroking the fake fur featured in children's activity books. Actively engaging with books—not just passively listening to the words—helps an infant develop a love of reading that can last a lifetime.

182 listen up!

In this auditory version of hide-and-seek, stand behind your baby while she's playing on the floor. Call out "Where's Mommy?" or "Where's Daddy?" then wait for her to turn around and locate you. When she goes back to playing, call out again from a different location behind her.

183 perform scarf tricks

You don't have to be a magician to pull off this trick—and you'll be helping your baby work on his fine motor skills and eye-hand coordination. Simply stuff a lightweight scarf into a paper-towel tube. Then—voilà!—show your baby how to pull it out. Now put it back in and let him tug it out himself.

184 make a family photo album

Strengthen the bond your baby feels with the rest of her family by filling an album with photos of people she knows and loves. Add pictures of beloved pets and toys, too, and you'll have a book that will engage and entertain her for years to come.

186 give her a security blanket

Many infants adopt what developmental psychologists call a "transitional object." It's usually a blanket or plush toy that gives a child something that—unlike people—doesn't come and go. So let your baby cling to, suck on, sleep with, and drag around her special object as much as she likes, since it provides a sense of continuity and reassurance.

185 hide sounds

Hide an object that makes noise—a ticking clock, a music box, or a talking plush toy—where your adventurous crawler can find it. As he searches for the source of the sound, he'll be testing his auditory tracking skills. He'll also gain a sense of mastery when he discovers the little noisemaker.

6+
months

188 play dropsie

As your infant gains more control of her hands and a better understanding of what they do, she'll discover the age-old game of dropsie. The rules are simple: baby drops an object on the floor; parent picks it up. Baby drops object again; parent picks it up again. Tedious, right? But look at it from your baby's point of view: she's showing you that she understands she has power over objects and can influence people's behavior—and that's a huge cognitive leap forward for babykind.

189 meet mr. knickerbocker

It will be a few more months before your baby can make all the sounds in this chant, but he'll love the rhythm and enjoy watching you go through the movements.
Hey, Mr. Knickerbocker, boppity bop!
pat your hands on the floor once, clap, repeat
I like the way you boppity bop!
continue patting and clapping to establish a beat
Listen to the sound we make with our hands.
rub your palms together
Listen to the sound we make with our feet.
stomp your feet on the floor to the beat
Listen to the sound we make with our knees.
tap your fingers on your knees to the beat
Listen to the sound we make with our teeth.
click your teeth together

187 fly a kite

Few toys are as magical to a child as a colorful kite soaring in the sky. While carefully supervising, allow your baby to touch the tugging string and see how it leads up to the dancing kite.

tip

Sometimes it's the old, traditional songs that have the most charm—invite the whole family to join in!

190 go jogging

Whether you're running or walking, you'll get great exercise pushing your baby in a jogging stroller, and she'll love feeling the wind in her hair. Wait until she's about six months old, when her neck muscles are strong enough to withstand the jostling. Use a stroller made for jogging; it will have better shock absorption.

191 introduce tactile treats

Whip up a batch of colored gelatin and place either cubes or spoonfuls on your child's highchair tray. Then watch as your aspiring artist creates abstract sculpture by smearing, rolling, squishing, squashing, and smashing the shimmering stuff.

192 babble with your baby

Have you noticed how your baby tends to say his "words" in a series, such as "ba-ba-ba" and "ma-ma-ma"? Expand his listening skills and sound repertoire by introducing him to new sounds, like "ta-ta-ta" and "la-la-la." Then wait for him to respond. You're starting to teach him the art of conversation!

193 devise a distraction

Rather than fight your baby's urge to grab things at the grocery store, give her a bag of marshmallows, a box of macaroni, or a carton of tofu to examine, squeeze, and shake while she sits in the shopping cart. The novelty of these impromptu "toys" will keep her happily occupied (while still under your watchful eye).

194 find the puppy

Put on a dog and pony show for your baby with this version of peekaboo. Show him a plush puppy, tuck it behind your back, and sing:

Oh where, oh where
Has my little dog gone,
Oh where, oh where can he be?
With his ears so short
And his tail so long,
Oh where, oh where can he be?

Then, with a "woof, woof," bring the dog back out again: "There he is!"

195 knock 'em down

Your baby is not old enough to construct block towers yet (that typically happens around 16 months of age), but he will enjoy using his hands to knock over structures that you build for him. The sight—and sound—of crashing blocks will entice your little demolition expert to do it repeatedly, so be prepared for a busy construction schedule!

196 turn to the flip side

Tape a bright, simple picture to a big, plain box and show it to your baby. Once you've engaged her attention, encourage her to find the picture by turning the box around. She might scoot or crawl around the box, chasing the picture that she watched you make disappear.

197 shake it up

To graduate beyond infant rattles, make "big-kid" noisemakers by filling plastic storage containers with assorted objects: jar lids, spoons, wooden blocks (nothing small enough to be a choking hazard). Snap on the lids securely and listen as he shakes, rattles, and rolls.

198 dine in the buff

Even the most adorable baby clothes lose their appeal when they're covered in cereal or puréed peas. So let your little diner eat in the buff once in a while. Not only will it keep her clothes stain-free, but it's also fun for her. And when she smears carrots across her chest, remember that she's becoming more aware of her body.

199 squeeze the sponges

Give your bathing beauty a variety of body scrubbers such as loofahs, bath mitts, and natural sponges to play with in the tub or a big basin of water. Squeezing water out of the sponges will stimulate his sense of touch and strengthen his small hands. (Always remember to closely supervise water play.)

200 add funny words

By about six months of age, babies have developed quite a sense of humor. Many can even appreciate simple word games: try adding a gorilla to the lyrics of "Old MacDonald," or singing "kitty" instead of "baby" in the song "Rock-a-Bye Baby"—and watch the smiles begin.

 tip *By encouraging listening skills you are helping your baby's later language development.*

201 crawl together

Many babies think it's hilarious to follow a crawling parent around the house or yard—so indulge your newly mobile explorer. (And by getting a baby's-eye view of the world, you may see safety hazards you hadn't noticed before.)

202 explore a fabric tunnel

A collapsible cloth tunnel (available at specialty toy stores) will tempt novice and experienced crawlers alike. Crawling through it will teach your baby about spatial relations, and if you add a toy inside, she'll discover that there's a prize at the end of the tunnel!

203 hide in plain sight

If your baby easily finds toys hidden under boxes or blankets, challenge his sense of perception by concealing a toy behind a transparent barrier, like a clear cutting board or a plastic picture frame. Does he try to get the toy by reaching through the cutting board or frame—or by reaching around it?

204 horse around with hats

Your baby's fascination with her own image will make her a rapt audience if you set her in front of a mirror and have her model some hats. Fancy ones are fun, but even a baseball cap or a straw gardening hat will do nicely.

6+ months

205 tease and tickle

This game introduces your baby to the names of body parts—and works well as a diaper-changing distraction.
Bug-a-boo's got feet, feet, feet
lightly tickle your baby's feet
Bug-a-boo's got shins
flutter your fingers up his legs
Bug-a-boo's got a mouth to eat
pat your fingers on his mouth
And Bug-a-boo's got chins!
give him a quick tickle under his chin

206 model sweet behavior

Your baby will model your behavior, even when the action is directed at, say, a teddy bear: "Here's a kiss for Teddy!" and "Here's a kiss for Baby!"

207 spray for fun

Babies love new sensations, and being sprinkled on the tummy with cooling drops of water is a particularly refreshing one. Use a clean squirt bottle to spray your baby with a fine mist of water.

208 teach him to feed himself

Do you spend more time trying to stop your baby from grabbing his spoon than actually feeding him with it? Then it's time to start letting him take over. Load a child-size spoon with a sticky food that won't slide off, such as oatmeal or thick rice cereal; put the spoon in his hand, and guide it to his mouth. He'll be feeding himself with a utensil on his own in the second year.

209 spoon it out

Raid your kitchen's utensil drawer for large spoons and spatulas that your baby can wave, bang, and lick. Show her how to pass a spoon from hand to hand, which will teach her how to grasp with one hand while releasing with the other—no small feat for a little one.

210 greet him on the fly

Next time you're pushing your baby on a playground bucket swing, enhance the physical fun by cheerfully saying "bye" when you push the swing up and reuniting with a happy "hi" when the swing comes back to you. He may not understand the words, but he'll notice the repeating sounds, and may kick his feet in anticipation of the next push of the swing.

211 bathe with buoyancy

Collect assorted floating objects—like waterproof toys and empty plastic bottles (tape caps securely shut)—and set the little flotilla adrift in the bathtub. Your little sailor will love watching them bobble and hearing you name and describe any objects she manages to catch. (Always supervise water play.)

214 make a book

Even at this tender age, babies begin to express their interests. One may be enamored of ducks, another of trees, and another of bananas. Indulge your baby's fancies by making a book about her favorite subject. Punch holes in several pieces of cardboard, string them together with yarn, and paste in pictures from magazines or even your own drawings. As she grows older, this type of book conveys the idea that a single thing can be portrayed in many different ways.

212 permit peaceful moments

In the hustle and bustle of life with a baby, it can be difficult to balance work, play, and exercise with quiet time. Try to indulge in peaceful moments with your child—whether you're sitting on the lawn listening to birds sing or just lying on the bed watching the ceiling fan spin around. Quiet time gives you and your baby a chance to relax and bond in a deeper way than when you're rushing between places and activities.

213 look up

Point out birds, butterflies, planes, and other winged wonders to your baby to elevate his perspective into the sky above his head.

215 meet the animals

You may not be ready to bring home a pet goldfish, guinea pig, puppy, or iguana, but your baby will love seeing the animal world in action. A well-stocked pet store can provide almost as much fun as a zoo, because babies are as captivated by a domestic mouse as they are by an African lion.

216 pull a switcheroo

Stand in front of your baby and hold a small puppet or plush toy behind your back. Bring it out in front of you and show it to your baby, using first your left hand, then your right, then your left again. Soon you'll be able to tell by his expectant gaze that he's anticipating which hand will have the toy. Try varying the pattern you follow. Can he anticipate that one, too?

217 kiss with gusto

Babies learn that kissing is a sign of affection, and they start kissing back at about eight months of age. Encourage your little smoocher by asking "Who wants a kiss? Who wants a kiss?" Then make an exaggerated sound as you plant one on his cheek.

218 tell stories

Hearing books read aloud is important for all kids—even those who are already reading on their own. But reading the printed words isn't enough. Expand your baby's vocabulary and introduce new ideas by talking about what's on the page, such as the various colors and shapes. This type of storytime discussion will engage your child for years to come.

219 try a new peekaboo

You and your baby have likely gotten hours and hours of pleasure from playing the classic game of peekaboo, in which you cover and uncover your face with your hands. Try a new version the next time you change your child's diaper: instead of hiding your face, place a clean diaper on your baby's face. When he reaches out to pull it off, help him remove it, and exclaim, "Peekaboo!" This game helps him understand that both you and he still exist even when he's "hiding."

220 row your boat

Take your baby for a make-believe boat ride to the tune of "Row, Row, Row Your Boat." Sit with your knees bent and your feet flat on the floor. Position your little sailor with her back against your tummy. Gently rock forward and back as you hold her hands and "row" together. The rocking will stimulate her vestibular system (which aids balance)—and work your abs!

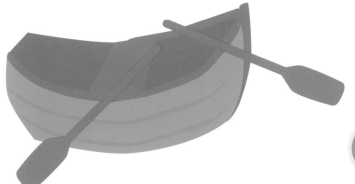

221 stock up

At age six months and up, babies develop a pattern: see, grab, and let go. Rather than chastising your curious one for doing what comes naturally, fill a low bin with items she has free license to explore by herself while you're nearby to watch. Stock toys, unused sponges, cups, or whatever is on hand that's safe and easy for her to handle.

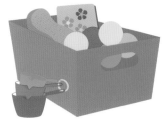

222 bend those knees

Even after your baby has mastered the fine art of pulling himself up to a standing position by holding onto the nearest object—be it an armchair or your leg—he may be unsure how to get back down on the floor. You may find his bewildered look adorable at first, but after he's called you over and over, it loses some of its charm. To teach him how to lower himself without falling, gently push behind his knees to make them bend. Then guide him down and slightly forward until he ends up on his knees. After a few days' practice, he'll be pulling himself up and plopping down with ease.

 tip *Laying your baby down and gently "cycling" his legs helps strengthen larger muscles needed for standing.*

6+ months

223 knock his socks off

It's inevitable: once your baby figures out how to pull off his stretchy little socks and expose his toes, he'll do it repeatedly. This activity gives him a precious sense of self-determination and helps build coordination. So applaud his efforts. As long as it's not cold, it's fine to bare those tootsies.

224 feel the fruit

You've just come in, and you need 10 minutes to put away the groceries. So plunk your little one down on the kitchen floor and present some play-worthy produce to engross her, within your field of vision, while you finish your task. She'll love how the rough-skinned cantaloupe and the sweet-smelling oranges roll in funny, unpredictable ways.

225 phone home

If your baby watches you intently during your phone conversations, let her in on the mystery. The next time you talk to a caller she knows well, put the phone up to her ear so she can hear that familiar voice. Soon she'll be ready to babble some replies.

226 record her voice

As your child starts to understand that she is actually a separate person (a concept that fully develops when she's 12 to 15 months old), hearing her own voice will thrill her. Record her gurgling, babbling, and giggling, then play it back for her. This also will give you an audio scrapbook of some of your baby's first sounds.

227 fill up the jar

Once your baby can sit up on his own, give him a plastic jar with an extra-wide mouth and some small, age-appropriate toys. Guide his hand and show him how to put the toys into the jar; this teaches him about spatial relations ("How much stuff fits in here?"). Demonstrating how to remove the toys boosts his problem-solving skills ("How can I get these toys out?").

228 go bottoms-up

Lie on your back, knees bent and feet flat on the floor, and lay your baby on your shins, facing you. Holding him snugly, curl your knees toward your nose until he's horizontal or slightly bottoms-up.

229 hide the balls

Put on a magic show for your baby by rolling some balls through a cardboard tube. He'll be fascinated as he watches the balls disappear—then suddenly reappear. This trick will also teach him about object permanence (the idea that an object doesn't cease to exist just because it's not visible) and spatial relations (the way some things, like balls, fit into other things).

230 make merry music

Music takes on new meaning when your baby learns about making it with other people (not just listening to it). Pick up a recorder or drum; hand him a tambourine or rattle. Even if you're only able to ting-ting a triangle, you'll both love the music that you make together.

231 present some pasta

Put a spoonful of cool, wet, cooked spaghetti on your baby's highchair tray. She'll enjoy trying to peel apart and squish the slippery strands.

232 say "thank you"

Her emerging awareness of social relations means that she'll get a kick out of the simple game of handing you toys and hearing you say "thank you" again and again. Besides entertaining her, this little ritual introduces her to a core concept of etiquette: expressing gratitude.

233 get wet

If the weather's warm enough, pour a shallow amount of water into a large tub or kiddie pool outside and let your baby splash around. Add small plastic watering cans, buckets, and rubber ducks for more fun—but never leave her alone, not even for a minute.

234 teach the sign for "drink"

Babies can learn signs long before they learn to speak. So teach your baby some signs, such as this one for "drink": curl your hand as if you are holding a cup and bring it to your lips. Or simplify the movement by making a fist and tapping your thumb on your lips. Make this motion every time you give your baby a drink. Soon she'll do it herself to show you that she's thirsty.

235 drum it up

Hold off on the drum set until your baby is a teenager—or at least until he can sit up by himself! In the meantime, let him pound away on other percussive objects, like saucepans and plastic containers. Early exploration of sound teaches him about rhythm.

236 hop for fun

She can't jump, she can't walk, and she may not even be sitting on her own yet, but your baby will be thrilled to hop up and down in a jumpy seat—and her legs will get stronger with each takeoff and landing. Clamp the seat onto an extra-wide door frame so she has room to move around, and stay nearby to ensure her safety.

237 feast on finger foods

Once your baby can feed himself, encourage him to practice this skill by laying out bite-sized morsels that you can enjoy together. This allows him to show off his all-important pincer grasp using his forefinger and thumb—and bask in a special meal just with you.

238 sing a song of teeth

Clean those emerging first teeth and surrounding gums with a wet thin washcloth, a piece of gauze, or a baby toothbrush—no need for toothpaste just yet. Introduce this cleaning routine in baby steps: open your own mouth wide to encourage imitation; then start with just one quick, shallow swipe in your baby's mouth. You can get more thorough as the action becomes familiar. Add some fun to the routine by singing this song to the tune of "Here We Go 'Round the Mulberry Bush":
This is the way we brush our teeth
Brush our teeth
Brush our teeth
This is the way we brush our teeth
So early in the morning!

239 switch on

Your baby is starting to learn about cause and effect. Allowing her to play with the lights, switching them on and off, on and off, will give her a great sense of power!

240 sock it away

Play with your baby's budding understanding of object permanence (the notion that an object exists even when it isn't visible) by placing a toy in an adult-size sock. Show him how you pull the toy out by reaching your hand inside the sock. Soon he'll begin to look in the sock for the missing toy himself.

241 give a juggling lesson

With a toy in each of her hands, what will your baby do if you offer her a third toy? Will she try to grab it with her hands full? Or drop everything? In time, she'll put down one toy before grasping another.

242 create a crawl course

Once your child masters the art of crawling, set up an easy obstacle course where she can hone her problem-solving abilities and practice the gross motor skills that her newly acquired mobility requires. Choose an area with a soft rug, or roll out a mat or blanket to cushion her hands and knees. Set up small cushions and piles of blankets for her to clamber over; be ready to give her a boost over obstacles if she needs it. Drape sheets over chairs to create tunnels to crawl through, and hide toys for her to discover along the way.

6+
months

243 describe the world

The more you talk, the more your baby will hear and the more words he'll store in his memory. Providing a running commentary on everyday life introduces him to the rhythms of speech. Through this, he'll begin to understand the world around him and how people explain things to each other. Someday you'll hear him telling his teddy something in the same tone you used to explain it to him—and you'll know he was listening.

6+ months

244 give her a hand

By six months, many infants are ready to learn to clap. Gently hold your baby's hands between yours and clap them together while chanting a nursery rhyme such as "Pat-a-Cake." Eventually she'll get the hang of the routine and start clapping on her own.

245 bang away

Set a metal, rimmed cookie sheet on the floor in front of your baby or on his highchair tray, then give him a selection of hard objects, such as wooden blocks, metal spoons, and plastic cups. Help him drop the objects onto the sheet. Which bang does he like best?

246 make a splash

The game of dropsie takes on a whole new meaning when you add water. Partially fill a bathtub, then give your baby waterproof toys and balls to drop into it. The resulting splash will delight her, and the actions she's performing will develop her eye-hand coordination, exercise her grasp-and-release skills, and demonstrate cause and effect. (Always supervise water play.)

tip *Think about the best way to babyproof your home to address your baby's increasing mobility.*

247 search for the baby

When you pull a shirt over your child's head, at the moment his face is hidden by the shirt, ask enthusiastically, "Where's the baby?" When his face reappears, say, "There he is!" Vary the game by lifting him over your head while you pretend to search for him, then bringing him face-to-face for a cheerful reunion.

248 vary your smooches

By now, your baby is old enough to see the joy in kisses that depart from the norm. Try an Eskimo kiss (rubbing noses), a butterfly kiss (fluttering your eyelashes against her cheek), and an angel kiss (kissing her eyelids). Before long, she'll be kissing you back in a variety of ways.

249 share a laugh

This is the age when babies start laughing at their own humor. The "joke" may be dropping a toy on the floor over and over, shrieking at passersby, or making open-mouthed faces. Whatever tickles your baby's fancy, let it tickle yours as well. Laughing at his jokes shows him that he has the power to amuse people.

6+ months

250 pop open an umbrella

Babies make an easy-to-impress audience. From your baby's viewpoint, for example, an umbrella mysteriously transforms—with a click and a swoosh—from a long, wrinkled object to a smooth, colorful expanse. So open an umbrella in front of her with a bit of drama and say, "Open sesame!" followed by a quick Mary Poppins–style twirl of the umbrella. You'll win her entertainer-of-the-year award!

9+ nine months & up

milestones

Your baby is building on her repertoire of skills and continues to learn through all her senses.

- She's starting to explore textures (smooth leaves, rough bark) and sounds (birds, music).

- Dropping her toys onto the floor from her highchair helps her learn about cause and effect.

- The idea that you're still there even when she can't see you (called object permanence) is a new development.

Your baby is starting to look and act more like a toddler. Listen for strings of babbling sounds that imitate sentences; your child understands many words that she can't yet say. Because mobility is her main aim, games that allow her to practice gross motor skills, such as crawling, appeal to her. Fine motor skills are important, too. She might insist on turning book pages or stacking blocks on her own. Get ready: this is the start of the do-it-myself stage.

251 get out the muffin pan

Once your baby has mastered the ability to pick up and release objects, he'll enjoy plopping tennis balls, toys, and wads of crumpled-up paper into the cups of muffin tins—an action that hones fine motor skills.

252 revisit the laundry basket

Chances are you already own one of the world's most versatile baby toys: the laundry basket. It makes a perfect fort, playpen, or doll crib. Your baby can also throw toys in it and push it around, or climb in and have you pull her across the floor. Someday you may even get to put laundry in the basket again!

253 give him a lift

Let your child experience the joy of motion with this up-in-the-air game. Sit on a carpeted floor with your baby facing you. Lift him up and, while holding him firmly, roll back so that he "flies" over your head. This action strengthens his back and stimulates the vestibular system, which helps him balance. It's also likely to prompt a lot of giggles from your copilot.

254 bring out the brushes

Water play in all forms (supervised, of course) will be a hit for years to come with your little one. On a warm afternoon, give her some dollar-store paintbrushes and a bucket of water, and let her "paint" the sidewalk.

255 challenge balancing skills

Kids love to test their balancing skills by trying to crawl or walk along wide beams in parks and at children's play centers. They can enjoy such balancing acts at home, too: simply lean a broad, firm board up against a low, sturdy chair or table. Make sure the floor underneath is cushioned. Then, as you stand beside him or hold his hand, encourage him to crawl or walk up and down the board.

256 introduce push toys

Even before she masters alternating her legs to propel herself on a riding toy, your child can push herself with both legs at once. This pushing action allows her to strengthen her muscles and experience the joy of independent mobility. Stay nearby, as your baby may still need a helping hand to keep her balanced and safe.

257 steer a baby wheelbarrow

This activity strengthens your child's upper body and helps develop his coordination: pick him up by his hips or under his chest so he can "walk" on his hands. When he's older and stronger, hold up his feet instead.

258 offer puppet kisses

Don a small hand puppet and use it to give "kisses" to different parts of your baby's body. She'll love to hear you tell her where the puppet is going to kiss her next.

259 play peekaboo with toys

Reinforce the concept of object permanence (the idea that objects exist even when they aren't visible) by making a big show of hiding a toy under a blanket and then helping your child find it. Soon he'll learn to recognize shapes by the hidden toy's outline—for instance, the telltale lump of his plush bunny. If he's having trouble finding the toy, cover just part of it.

260 master the stairs

Although it's tempting to turn stairs into a forbidden zone, it's better to teach your baby how to navigate them safely. Climbing up doesn't take much practice, but to go down safely, she needs to turn onto her belly and lower her feet down onto each step. Once she learns how to feel for a solid object behind her feet, she'll have the foundation not only for stair-climbing but also for later pursuits, such as scrambling around a play structure. Always make sure the safety gates are closed when your baby is not practicing her climbing under your supervision.

261 stuff a box

Cut a large hole in the lid or side of a shoe box, then show your baby how to stuff toys through the hole and into the box. He'll learn about the relative sizes of toys and about object permanence. Picking up and pushing toys through the hole will also help him develop his fine motor skills.

tip *Putting items into a box and pulling them out helps develop your baby's sense of spatial relations.*

262 sort the shapes

With a shape-sorter toy, first show your child how the round piece fits into the round hole, then show him how the square and triangular pieces fit into their matching holes. Soon he'll be matching up the shapes himself. This activity teaches spatial relations and shape discrimination, and develops fine motor skills.

263 draw together

It will be a few years before your baby can draw anything even remotely resembling, well, anything. Still, she'll enjoy drawing lines with a crayon, marker, or piece of chalk. If she can't do it herself, hold her hand gently in yours and guide it on the paper.

264 seek stability

You can use a large vinyl stability ball (sold at sporting-goods stores) to stimulate and help strengthen your child's sense of balance, which is crucial for learning how to walk and, in time, how to run. Seat him on top of the ball and, holding his torso, gently bounce him from side to side or roll the ball back and forth.

265 encourage early walkers

The primary challenge of walking is finding one's balance. To help your toddler-to-be get up—and stay up—give her objects that provide resistance and stability but are light enough for her to push. A laundry basket filled with clothes works well. Avoid baby walkers and tricycles, however, as they roll too quickly.

266 build a house

An older baby's love of child-sized spaces, the peekaboo game, and imitative play means that he'll be thrilled to have his own house—be it ever so humble. Get a big box from an appliance store, cut out windows and a door, and decorate the exterior with paint and stickers. Tuck blankets and toys inside to create a cozy retreat for the new tenant.

267 smell intriguing scents

Gather some small plastic containers, such as clean yogurt cups, and look in your pantry for some strongly scented ingredients to insert inside each container. For example, saturate a cotton ball with vanilla extract or crumple a cinnamon stick. Put one ingredient into each container, close and tape it securely shut, then poke holes in the lid. Let your baby sniff the scents.

268 soar down the slide

At first, your baby may want to go down the kiddie slide only with your help—guiding her from the side and catching her at the end. Over time, however, as she feels safer, she'll want to whiz down all by herself.

269 sing for supper

Recite this rhyme as your baby enjoys his food:
Sippity sup, sippity sup,
Bread and milk from a china cup.
Bread and milk from a bright silver spoon,
Made of a piece of the
bright silver moon.
Sippity sup, sippity sup,
Sippity, sippity, sup!

270 play hide-and-seek

For months, your baby has been experimenting with the concept of object permanence (the notion that objects exist even when they aren't visible). Now she is finally ready for the big time: a game of hide-and-seek, where both baby and grown-up get to do the hiding and the seeking. But don't do a really good job of hiding, because that might frustrate or scare your baby. Instead, help her by calling out, "Come find me! Where am I?" This game isn't just fun for babies—it also helps them work through separation anxiety as they see you "return" after your "disappearances."

271 explore the world on foot

If your baby's walking, provide him with plenty of opportunities to amble down the sidewalk, meander along a dirt path, or waddle across a grassy lawn. He sharpens his powers of observation as he picks up rocks and sticks, listens to his shoes tapping on the concrete, and stops to examine scurrying bugs.

272 burst the bubbles

Your baby has always loved to watch you blow soap bubbles, and at about nine months of age, she's now ready to reach out and pop them. So encourage her! She'll practice her eye-hand coordination—and she will feel proud of her popping performance.

273 talk into a tube

If your child is intrigued by sounds—especially the funny ones he makes himself—then talking (or rather, babbling) through a tube might be a lot of fun for him. Pick up a paper-towel or wrapping-paper tube and show him how to talk, blow, hum, and sing through it. Then let him take a turn.

274 give her a backpack

When she sees an older sibling—or another adult—using a backpack, your little one will probably want to have one, too. Although she can't wear a pack until she's a steady walker, she'll enjoy helping you fill her personal pack with toys, snacks, or books—and then dumping them out again.

275 dial his number

Fascinated by the ringing and all the buttons, your baby may already be grabbing for your phone. End the power struggle by giving him one of his own. Whether it's a toy or an unwanted cordless phone (with the battery removed), pretending to use it will make him feel like Mommy or Daddy. At the same time, he'll get to practice his language and social skills.

276 take turns

Your child will jump at the chance to practice walking by pulling or pushing a sturdy wagon. Take turns with her: first give her a ride in the wagon, then have her give her small charges (dolls and plush toys) a ride.

 tip *Learning to alternate her legs while pushing a wagon full of blocks is great walking practice for your baby.*

277 stack the rings

Your child won't be able to stack colored rings on a plastic toy pole in order from large to small until he's closer to age two. At this stage, urge him to use his budding problem-solving skills and eye-hand coordination to stack the rings in any order—and to enjoy what he does best now: take things apart!

278 wave bye-bye

Saying good-bye is one of the first social rituals babies learn because it's a gesture they can easily recognize and copy. By teaching your child about language ("bye-bye!") and routines (the action of waving every time someone leaves), you establish a soothing ritual that might help her if separation anxiety is making departures difficult.

279 visit the zoo

If your baby crows over animals seen in the distance and in books, seek opportunities for him to see new species and perhaps even touch some live critters. Visit a pet store or petting zoo to introduce him to some of the amazing creatures that inhabit our planet. Be sure to supervise your little one's interspecies meeting, and wash his hands afterward.

9+ months

280 play jack-in-the-box

This old-fashioned toy, with its tinkling tune and pop-up puppet, continues to delight kids, even the very young. Help your baby turn the handle and stuff the puppet back into the box after it pops up—but no one needs to teach her how to laugh when that puppet magically greets her again and again!

281 get cheeky

In the realm of simple baby pleasures, squashing a parent's puffed-out cheeks between two hands ranks high, especially if you act very surprised each time your baby does it.

282 cut to the chase

Whether he's zipping around on all fours or waddling around on two feet, your baby will love an active game of chase. Keep it gentle—you don't want to frighten him—but motivate him with words of encouragement, funny noises, and lots of laughter. Then change it around so he gets to chase you, too.

283 take a dip

And she thought her little bathtub was fun! From the safety of your arms, your little swimmer can learn to feel comfortable in the wide-open space of a pool. Bounce through the water together while she revels in the sensation of weightlessness and discovers the joy of kicking and splashing. (Never leave your child unattended in or near a pool.)

284 bathe the toy babies

Set up a small tub with warm water and soap suds to give your baby a chance to bathe his own "babies," whether they're dolls, rubber duckies, or plastic dinosaurs. Remember to supervise him at all times, and keep a towel on hand for spills.

285 pour another one

Your baby sees you pouring liquids all day long: a cup of coffee for yourself, some breast milk or formula into her bottle, or water into the cat's bowl. From her perspective, this looks like a lot of fun. So give her a turn: when she's in the tub, let her practice pouring with plastic cups and bottles. She'll develop an awareness of size and volume while sharpening her fine motor skills. (Never leave a child alone in a tub.)

 tip *Keep a stock of towels nearby so spills from water play don't become a slipping hazard.*

286 bedazzle with balloons

Show your baby colorful helium-filled balloons and demonstrate how tugging on their strings makes the balloons dance and bob in the air. Always choose Mylar balloons—never latex ones, which are a choking hazard if popped. Closely supervise balloon play at all times and make sure that the strings are short enough that your baby can't get tangled in them.

287 give encouragement

Praise—in the form of "You're such a good girl!" or "What a smart girl!"—generally focuses on the child herself. Encouragement, on the other hand, is aimed at a child's efforts: "You really worked hard to get up that hill!" or "I'm amazed at how fast you can run!" Most experts agree that encouraging a child is preferable to praising her, because praise sets the child up for wanting to always be "smart," "good," or "strong," whereas encouragement focuses on the child's actions and not her worth as a person. Start boosting your baby's sense of competence now, as she's becoming aware of herself as a separate being who needs to be recognized as both lovable and capable.

288 get tools for tots

Older babies and toddlers are keenly interested in imitating the grown-ups in their lives, so you might find your little one trying to sweep up crumbs or bang a hammer. Keep him safe yet satisfied by giving him toy versions of the tools you use around the house. Whether he's fiddling in a play kitchen or puttering in a pretend workshop, this initial imitating behavior will evolve into full-fledged fantasy play later on, in which armchairs serve as pirate ships and leaves are ingredients for a magic potion.

9+ months

289 wrap her up

Unroll about 4 feet (1.2 m) of wrapping paper on the floor and plop your baby in the middle of it. She'll enjoy rolling on it, tearing it, crackling it, and pulling it across her body. Just make sure she doesn't tear off any pieces and put them in her mouth, as they could pose a choking hazard.

290 bring rattles

Even though your baby has outgrown his infant toys, the rattles can delight him in new, exciting ways. Make a game by hiding them in a shoe box, assembling a rattle "band," or stacking them up.

291 ride a rocking horse

Your little cowgirl will love rocking herself back and forth on a plastic pony or classic wooden steed. Set the horse on plush carpet or grass and always stand by, just in case the bronco bucks.

292 puzzle it out

Exercise your baby's spatial-relation and fine motor skills with durable wooden puzzles. Start with a basic circle-shaped puzzle with only one piece; once he masters that, graduate to a puzzle with a few more pieces. Look for easy-to-grasp knobs, bright colors, and matching pictures or patterns on the board that will help him determine where each piece goes. Show him how to slide the pieces into place.

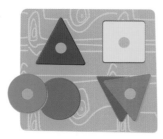

293 reverse the roles

At about nine months, babies start imitating the grown-ups and older kids in their lives and enjoy giving them some personal attention. So encourage your child to put food in your mouth, dab your face with a washcloth, and brush your hair. It makes her feel like a big person and allows her to be the nurturer, not just the one being nurtured.

294 broaden your circle

Schedule get-togethers with other parents and babies. Even though your baby won't play directly with other children until he's near the end of his second year, he'll enjoy watching and imitating them. And you'll learn from observing other babies—and parents, too!

295 give her a foot rub

Feet are wonderfully sensitive to touch. Treat your active baby to a relaxing foot massage before she goes to bed. Softly rub the bottom of each toe, then make circular movements on her heels with your thumbs. For a more soothing massage, use a child-safe lotion.

296 record a book on tape

When you leave your child with a babysitter, let him know you're still thinking about him no matter where you are by recording yourself reading one of his favorite books. He'll love hearing your voice when you're not there and listening to the story's familiar words. For nap time, record several books in a row for him to listen to as he falls asleep.

298 grab for gadgets

Your baby is at the peak age for seeking out everyday objects, such as cups, plastic hangers, and boxes. These simple household items are just as effective as top-of-the-line developmental toys for practicing his fine motor skills and indulging in imitative play.

9+ months

297 teach her rhythm

Research shows that babies can perceive rhythms and anticipate what comes next in a pattern, even if they can't always replicate that pattern. Try this yourself by demonstrating a simple rhythm, like clap-clap-rest, clap-clap-rest. Watch as your baby tries to imitate this rhythm. Pattern recognition is key for learning to talk, read, do math, and appreciate music.

299 play at the beach

With plenty of sun protection and supervision, the beach makes a wonderful destination for you and your baby. He can dig in the sand, slap the water, watch the birds, and go for a dip—in an adult's arms, of course.

300 give blanket rides

A blanket ride is much like a sled ride, except that you pull a blanket across a floor or grass instead of a sled across snow. Sit or lay your child on a blanket, then gently and slowly pull the blanket. Try different directions. If you add an older child to the mix, she can ensure that the baby doesn't topple over, plus this doubles the fun!

301 elaborate on his past

Talking about what has happened in the past helps build your baby's capacity to remember. But don't just talk about common occurrences or ask questions with "yes" or "no" responses, such as "Did you have a yummy snack today?" Instead, elaborate on activities and relationships. For example, each day, talk about what you did together, where you went, and the people you saw: "When we played with your friend Carter at the park, a big black dog licked your toes!" In time, as you repeat the more memorable stories, your child will begin to build what psychologists call an "autobiographical memory."

302 stack the containers

Show your baby how to balance different-sized plastic containers on top of each other, and how to nest the small containers inside the big ones. This activity teaches spatial relations and how to discriminate between various shapes and sizes. Remember, he'll knock things down before he learns to stack them.

303 explore texture

Everyday objects often make the best toys, and each of them feels different to the touch. Gather a selection of items with unusual surface textures—bumpy, smooth, rough, slippery—and encourage your child to compare how they feel.

304 read it one more time

Familiarity breeds contentment in babies, even if the same old same old gets a little, well, old for grown-ups. Try to stay cheerful even if you've read that board book about trains 101 times in the last two weeks. The repetition helps your baby associate words with pictures, an essential step in developing both language and reading skills. And knowing what's coming on the next page makes her feel secure.

305 enjoy magical magnets

Place a variety of large, colorful magnets on the bottom portion of your refrigerator door or on a magnetic board. Together with your child experiment with sliding the magnets around, pulling them off, putting them back on, and stacking them up. Be sure to avoid small magnets, which can pose a choking hazard, and put the magnets away when you're done.

9+ months

306 shuffle the magic cups

A slower, simpler version of the classic shell game can be challenging and fun for babies. Show your child that you're putting a small toy or ball under a plastic cup. Then turn over a second cup. Slowly move the cups around. Now ask him to find the toy. He may not get it right away, but if you move the cups very slowly, eventually your baby will be able to guess correctly. (You might try playing with only one cup first to help him understand the game.)

 tip *Play games that involve moving a toy—slowly—to help strengthen your baby's visual tracking skills.*

307 massage her head

When your little one is in a quiet mood, pamper her with a head massage. Gently stroke her face along the bridge of her nose, then across her brows to her temples. Next, stroke from her nose across her cheeks. Finish by massaging along the sides of her face, including her ears, and finally the back of her head. Repeat this if she's enjoying your tender touch.

308 rearrange the furniture

The cruising phase—when babies hang on to furniture or human legs for support as they shuffle from one spot to another—is crucial in learning to walk. Help your child cruise by creating a chain of sturdy furniture that runs from one side of the room to the other. Move fragile objects, such as lamps, wobbly end tables, or plant stands, away from her eager grasp. Most babies go through the cruising stage relatively quickly. And her glee at being able to get around on her own two feet will make the disruption to your furniture well worth it.

309 show her yellow

As your child learns to sort objects by characteristics, color becomes increasingly important. Try having a yellow day: point out all the yellow objects you see. Green, orange, and purple days are sure to follow.

310 let 'er rip!

Before you toss out your magazines, let your baby explore the thrill of tearing out the pages! The ripping action sounds great and helps him develop both gross and fine motor skills. Make sure he doesn't put any paper in his mouth.

311 hide the toy

Tie a long ribbon onto a favorite small toy, then let your baby watch as you hide the tethered plaything under the sofa. Help her pull the ribbon to bring the toy back into view. Can she retrieve the toy by herself?

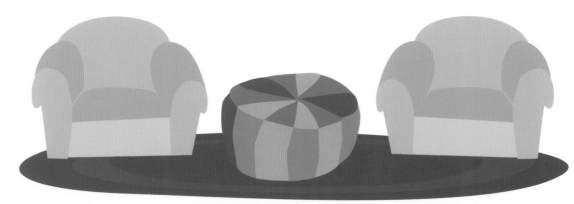

312 sing the color song

Help your baby learn about basic colors by singing this song as you point out examples of each color, like the red sock, the green ball, and the very blue fish.

Red and orange, green and blue
Shiny yellow and pink, too.
I love colors, and I love you!

313 flip some lids

Let your baby practice his manual-dexterity skills on a couple of large plastic storage jars with screw-top lids. Start by just resting a lid on top of a jar. Show him how to screw the lid on and off, and then let him try it.

314 run interference

Can't keep your baby from reaching into the wastebasket or unrolling the toilet paper? Remove temptations as much as possible (perhaps use a specialized toilet-paper holder). Try saying "no" to the undesired behavior just once or twice, then distract her with something equally intriguing. If she's digging in the trash, hand her a basket of toys to search through.

315 crawl and climb

Crawling and climbing are similar cross-lateral movements—one is horizontal and the other vertical. At the park, show your baby how to navigate interesting surfaces such as wide steps and short ladders by holding him firmly and guiding his hands and feet in the right direction. Don't let him try this alone, though!

316 invite toys to tea

Once your baby learns the purpose of using a cup, demonstrate how to give her teddy bear or doll an occasional "sip" of her water or (pretend) tea. She may laugh or even copy this bit of make-believe—a small precursor of all the imaginative play ahead.

9+ months

317 water plants together

Your baby loves to imitate you, and he's fascinated with water. So what better way to amuse him than by letting him water some outdoor plants? Hold his hands on a watering can or, for even more fun, use a hose. Of course, most of the water will go on his feet (and yours) and not on the plants, but he'll enjoy feeling like a big person—and getting a bit wet!

318 build a sand castle

He'll need help making the basic structure, but your young architect can pack a pail full of sand all by himself or just pile on handfuls of the stuff. The tactile stimulation of sand is irresistible, and the teamwork sets the foundation for future cooperative play.

319 point out the body parts

Share this classic children's song with your baby by demonstrating the movements as you sing. Then repeat the song and help her focus on her own body parts by guiding her hands to the appropriate places.

Head, shoulders, knees, and toes
touch your hands to these body parts in order
Knees and toes!
pat your knees and toes
Head, shoulders, knees, and toes
touch your hands to these body parts in order
Knees and toes!
pat your knees and toes
Eyes and ears and mouth and nose
touch your hands to these body parts in order
Head, shoulders, knees, and toes
touch your hands to these body parts in order
Knees and toes!
pat your knees and toes

320 teach "simon says"

Your baby's too young to play this game by the rules of the playground set. But a simplified version will teach him to listen to verbal directions and organize his body in order to follow them. Use simple commands at first, such as "Simon says touch your toes" or "Simon says open your mouth." Always demonstrate what you want your baby to do so he can try to imitate you.

321 revel in quiet reading

Reading to your little one is crucial for developing her love of books. And if she is showing even the slightest interest in looking at books alone, let her enjoy them on her own. It shows that she can entertain herself and that her attention span is increasing.

322 pair up shoes

Turn that jumble of shoes in your entryway or closet into a learning experience. Hand one shoe to your baby and ask her to help you find its mate. Start with one pair; as your baby masters the game, add more.

323 pedal away

When your baby reaches his first year, he's ready for the thrill of joining you on a bicycle ride—as long as he's wearing a helmet and sitting snugly in an approved child's seat or trailer. Travel on bike paths or well-paved roads with minimal traffic, and stop often to talk about the sights—and to check on him.

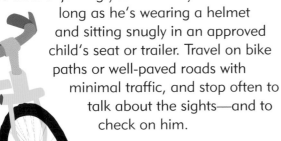

326 take a new route

An obstacle course can help your toddler develop balance and eye-foot coordination. Arrange small blocks or a broom handle to crawl or step over, hula hoops to go in and out of, a jump rope laid out in a wavy pattern to follow, and cushions to clamber over. Give her a hand if she needs one: the point is to help her develop as a walker, not to test her.

9+
months

324 wrap old favorites

Your baby might enjoy seeing some old friends. If you loosely wrap a few of her old favorite toys in wrapping paper, her play can start with crinkling the paper and ripping it open. (Just don't let it become a snack!)

325 play ball

Balls are an all-time favorite toy. Give your child a variety of different-sized balls and notice how she adapts her play for each one. Demonstrate the possibilities: throwing, rolling, bouncing, catching.

327 visit a museum

9+ months

Your inquisitive child will marvel at the colors and forms on display in an art museum. And the halls between galleries are great for practicing early walking skills. Avoid peak hours—and break up the art tour with visits to a café and the outdoors so he doesn't get bored or overstimulated.

328 say "good night"

To ease bedtime transitions, walk around the house with your baby saying good night to familiar objects: "Good night, teddy bear. Good night, blue couch. Good night, yellow toothbrush. Good night, Mommy's bed," and so on. This creates a soothing ritual for your baby and helps expand her vocabulary.

329 touch and talk

Help your baby develop tactile awareness. Fill a large, wide-mouthed plastic jar with items that have a very distinctive feel, like a plush dog, a plastic fish, and a rubber ball. As your baby enjoys pulling each object out of the jar, talk about what he's touching: "This dog is so soft!" and "Does that fish feel funny?"

330 walk tall

Congratulate your aspiring little walker with this charming song about one of life's most amazing milestones. Sing it to the tune of "I'm a Little Teapot."
I'm a little walker, I walk tall.
Sometimes I stumble, sometimes I fall.
But now I'm two-legged, so hear me call:
"I'm walking tall and having a ball!"

331 do broom pull-ups

To strengthen your baby's hands, arms, upper torso, and back, hold a broomstick horizontally in front of her, have her grasp the stick with both hands, then slowly lift her a few inches off the ground (so she doesn't fall far if she lets go). At first she may not be able to hold on, but after some practice your little gymnast may be able to suspend herself at least partially. Do this exercise over a soft surface, such as a large floor pillow.

332 play with pretend food

Given your baby's emerging interest in imaginative play and his budding ability to feed himself, try having a pretend meal with him, using plastic food and utensils. Choose large pieces of "food" that don't pose a choking hazard.

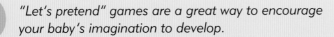

tip *"Let's pretend" games are a great way to encourage your baby's imagination to develop.*

333 remember the first words

Whether he says "aye" for hi, "oggo" for go, or "ope" for toast, make a list—or even a recording on a video camera—of your baby's first words. It will bring back sweet memories for you and your family in later years—and delight him when he's older, too!

334 put on a show

Puppet shows can be an effective tool for demonstrating how conversations work, whether they are between a puppet and your baby or among the puppets themselves—or both. These shows can also model appropriate expressions of emotions. As your child gets older, she may want to speak through the puppets and have them say things she'd be afraid to say herself. Encourage the dialogue.

12+
months

12+

twelve months & up

milestones

Your baby is becoming a toddler, maybe even taking her first steps with support.

• She knows and responds to her name and is also beginning to say more and more words.

• She can remember where her toys are, because her long-term memory is developing.

• As she points things out to you throughout the day, she is encouraging you to share her perspective.

Your child begins her second year as a great scientist, a fearless explorer, and an increasingly independent person. She is starting to recognize herself in the mirror and enjoys being in the company of other children. She loves achieving goals—even something as simple as opening and closing boxes—for the sheer joy of making things work. She's learning that there's a world out there beyond your lap, and she can't wait to experience everything in it.

335 pour it on

Offer your child a shallow tray of dry cereal and a paper or plastic cup. Have him watch as you fill the cup with cereal, then let him dump the cereal back into the tray. It's a physics lesson and a snack all in one.

338 blow some berries

When you combine a "raspberry" with a kid's belly, you've created one of the greatest sensory experiences a toddler can have. With your little one standing in front of you or lying on his back, pull up his shirt to bare his tummy, gently hold both of his hands, and blow a raspberry right against his belly. He'll giggle when you do it lightly, but you might want to experiment with using more gusto, too. Chances are excellent that the noisier you get, the harder he'll laugh.

336 track the train

This simple fingerplay gets 'em laughing every time.
The little train goes up the track.
walk your fingers up one of your child's arms from hand to shoulder
It says, "Choo, choo!"
tug gently at your child's earlobe
And then goes back.
walk your fingers back down your child's arm and make sure the train takes a trip up the other arm, too

339 finger-paint bags

Finger paints are wonderful fun for children at this age—and even more so when young artists can easily display the results of their efforts. Take a brown paper bag or any paper shopping bag with handles and cut it so that you have two flat surfaces, each with its own handle. Encourage your child to decorate the paper using nontoxic, child-safe finger paints, giving her free reign to get as creative and messy as she likes. When the paint is dry, hang her creations on doorknobs or drawer pulls to display her art at her eye level.

337 reach out for fun

Attach a couple of favorite toys to your child's car seat with short lengths of ribbon or plastic activity links. That way, they're at her fingertips for drive-time play.

340 push and pull

Sit on the floor with your little one, face-to-face with legs spread and the soles of his feet touching the insides of your legs to form a diamond shape. Join hands and do a gentle back-and-forth stretch. Lean back slowly (but not too far), pulling him toward you, then switch who does what, letting him pull you as he leans backward. Finish by leaning in toward each other and sharing a kiss.

341 mimic like monkeys

Little ones love to play "Monkey See, Monkey Do." Take turns mirroring each other's simple actions such as touching your nose and hiding your eyes, but keep the game from going on too long by using a code word to mark the end. How about "bananas"?

342 create page-turners

Make turning the pages of board books easier for little fingers. Punch holes at the top of each page, thread them with yarn, then tie the yarn off and trim the excess. The yarn bumps separate pages so your child can easily find the delights hidden within.

343 bang a pot

Let your toddler rock out in the kitchen with pots, pans, and metal measuring spoons to clink and clang together. Vary the sizes and shapes to help him achieve different sounds. Does a box with metallic tabs on it make an interesting noise?

12+
months

344 inspire exploration

Explore a one-year-old's favorite concepts—open and shut, in and out—with supervised access to a variety of easy-to-open jars and lidded containers filled with toys (nothing small enough to swallow, though). Learning to remove a lid, even one that's already unscrewed or partially opened, helps your toddler develop her fine motor skills and coordination.

 tip *Devote one shelf in the kitchen to your child, filling it with her toys and safe cookware to play with.*

345 buzz a fingerplay

Sit facing your child as you do this buzzy fingerplay.
Here is a beehive.
clasp your hands tightly together
Where are the bees?
hold your open hands out, palms up
Hidden away where nobody sees.
fold your arms across your chest
Soon they will come, flying out from the hive,
shade your eyes with your hand and peer out
One, two, three, four, five!
hold up your fists and open your fingers one by one
Buzzzzzzzzzzzz! Buzzzz!
with both of your hands up, flutter your fingers

346 do a hat trick

Take a medium-sized paper grocery bag and help your child decorate it with nontoxic crayons; leave the top 6 inches (15 cm) of the bag undecorated. When you're done, fold up the open end—a funny hat!

347 scope out the haircutter

Your toddler is more likely to take her first haircut in stride if she tags along on your hairdresser visits now. Make it a positive event—sit her in the tall chair and let her admire her own reflection in the big mirror.

348 further your yoga practice

Get out some yoga mats or beach towels, take off your shoes, put on soothing instrumental music, grab a yoga book or DVD, and start stretching together. Keep it fun, so the focus is on play more than exercise. Don't worry about perfect technique or holding poses for more than a few seconds. Your child may enjoy yoga poses that mimic animals, such as Downward-Facing Dog, Cobra, or Cat. Finish with the Happy Baby pose—the two of you can take turns being the baby!

349 play with laundry

Toddlers love to help. When you're sorting clean laundry, let your child pile socks or underwear into a drawer or stack towels into a laundry basket. This playful task gives him a chance to use his hands for grasping and sorting, and it will make him feel like a useful member of the household team.

352 expand musical horizons

Add songs that aren't strictly kids' tunes to your child's music library. Toddlers love lighthearted tunes like "Surfin' Safari" and "Octopus's Garden," and will respond well to most types of music. Mix what you love—jazz, country, rock, or pop—into the rotation of little-kid classics, and involve your child by dancing with him, singing along, and clapping out rhythms. Soon he'll have his own favorites, and one day you may hear one on the radio and he'll gleefully yelp, "They're playing my song!"

12+ months

350 go crackers about art

Invite your child to "finger paint" on graham crackers with yogurt or pudding. When she's done admiring it, she can eat her artwork.

351 start stacking

Now's the time for your child to begin experimenting with stacking blocks. Start with small stacks and react to collapses with a light "Uh-oh!" to avoid frustration.

353 float your boat

Fill a dishpan with water at room temperature (outdoors, you can use a kiddie pool) and throw in a dozen walnuts in their shells. Add a plastic cup and a strainer with a handle for scooping up the walnuts. Give your child's budding imagination some room here—are those floating things the Walnut People? Fish in the sea? Boats? Caution: walnuts will stain some bathtubs and sinks, so rather than trying this in the bath, use a pan you won't mind discoloring. And always supervise water play and empty the dishpan or pool when you're done.

354 shake it up

Have your child provide background "music" when you're hanging out together in the kitchen. Put some cereal in a large plastic sealable container, close it up, and let him shake away. For variety, give him wooden spoons to bang together or drum on the cereal shaker.

355 start the day right

Routines give kids a soothing sense of continuity and predictability. A morning routine can gear your child up for the day ahead and, if it ends with one or both parents heading off to work, prepares her for the separation. So greet the day with a morning song, do stretches together, or go for a short walk to check the weather and retrieve the newspaper.

356 pull my blanket

Seat plush animals in the middle of a blanket or throw rug and let your child pull them around the room. Then let him ride while you pull (gently and slowly).

 tip *Look at everyday things (squashy cushions, empty boxes) in a new light: they make fun playthings, too.*

357 sleep under the stars

Place glow-in-the-dark star stickers on the ceiling above your toddler's bed. Make sure the lights have been on awhile before bedtime so the stars absorb enough light to give off a comforting glow in the dark.

358 drop some clothespins

Select a wide-mouthed container such as an empty oatmeal carton, and offer it to your child along with some wooden clothespins (the old-fashioned kind without springs). She'll love putting the clothespins in and taking them out. Before long, she'll be standing and dropping in the pins from above, too.

359 bounce on a knee

Try out this lively multicharacter knee ride, increasing your bouncing tempo for faster and faster riders.
This is the way the farmer rides—walk, walk, walk.
This is the way the children ride—trot, trot, trot.
This is the way the lady rides—a-canter, a-canter.
This is the way the knight rides—a-gallop, a-gallop.
And whoa!
dip your little rider between your knees

360 share the social niceties

Understanding the social codes that help us get along with others will make your toddler feel like he's part of the adult world. So teach him to say "please" and "thank you" from the beginning, perhaps by playing games of handing objects back and forth. And it's important to say these words to him, too!

361 join the club

Waving good-bye, which most toddlers have learned to do by this age, both demonstrates and allows your child to practice important motor and social skills. Not only is waving good-bye an impressive feat of coordination; it's also like joining humanity's big social club by knowing the secret handshake.

362 look in the mirror

Toddlers love mirrors. Ask your child, "Who's that girl in the mirror?" Watch how she reacts as you talk to her about her mirror image. Ask, "Where's the girl's nose?" If she touches her own nose instead of pointing to the mirror, she's starting to identify herself as a unique person.

363 learn about leaves

Collect leaves from your yard or a nearby park. Look at them together, studying their shapes and structures. In autumn, place dry leaves in a basket or plastic container and let your child feel, smell, and crunch them. In the spring, look for new leaves just unfolding from their buds. Open up a bud to show your child the "baby" leaf forming inside.

364 get some kitchen help

Give your toddler simple tasks to do while you're in the kitchen together. He may enjoy putting wooden spoons in a plastic jar or oranges in a basket. Even if he isn't actually helping, he'll be practicing his eye-hand coordination and gaining a sense of accomplishment as he completes his task.

365 march like a mallard

Chant and march to work off kiddie energy on rainy days.
Little ducky Duddle went swimming in a puddle,
A puddle, a puddle quite small.
He said, "It doesn't matter
How much I splish and splatter.
I'm only a ducky after all!"

366 fly like a plane

Hold your arms straight out at your sides and buzz around the room, making sounds like an airplane. If your child is walking, she can imitate your movements and noises. If she's not quite walking yet, have her sit in front of you and mimic you as you bank your arms up and down. At the very least, you'll get her laughing at your silly antics!

367 cook a pancake

Make faces in pancakes by using berries or chocolate chips, and ask your child to name the nose, eyes, and mouth as you add them. Don't automatically offer sweet syrup—he may be perfectly happy without it.

368 crown me!

Make a crown for toddler royalty by cutting slits in the middle of a paper plate—first two perpendicular slits that cross the center of the plate, then two more crossing these to create eight equally spaced points on the plate. Have your child color the plate with nontoxic markers or crayons, then bend the points so they stand up around the rim. Now stage a coronation.

tip *Letting your child be the powerful ruler now and again helps boost his self-esteem.*

369 get a sinking feeling

Fill a dishpan (or a kiddie pool, in warm weather) with water and, making sure you're always supervising, bring out items for your child to experiment with. Does a cork float? How about a potato? Try lots of different toys and household objects, and sort them according to what happens when they hit the water.

370 teach a merry melody

Chances are that by this age your child has a few favorite tunes that are staples in her repertoire. Spend a morning singing these favorites with her a few times; then, while you hum the melodies, encourage her to sing the words. Or try leaving off the last few lyrics and have her finish the tune.

371 tuck baby in bed

Help your child make a snuggly bed for a doll or a plush animal using a shoe box and some of his smaller baby blankets. When it's nap time or bedtime, help him tuck in the "baby" before he gets tucked in himself.

372 take piggy farther

Just about every toddler relishes playing "This Little Piggy." To get more mileage out of the game, try drawing out the last line: "And this little piggy—that's right, this one, no, not that one, not that one, but this very little piggy right here on the end, oh yes, this little piggy— cried 'Whee, whee, whee,' all the way home!"

373 comfort her

When your toddler is cranky or just out of sorts, get her back on track by pulling her into your lap for a hug and a kiss. Your support helps her face the world—or at least that puzzle—again.

374 relax at mealtime

A child who doesn't always clear his plate is learning to listen to his body and stop eating when he's had enough. It's perfectly normal for your child to go through some periods when he can't be bothered to consume more than a few bites, and some when he eats everything that isn't nailed down. You might prepare an alternative if you're serving something he doesn't like, but it definitely isn't necessary—or a good idea—for you to become a short-order cook to make sure he eats enough.

375 name body parts

Once your child can point to body parts like her ears, eyes, and legs, ask her to call out the names of those body parts as you touch them. Ask, "What's this?" then reinforce her reply by saying, "That's right. That's your nose." Then turn the tables and ask, "So where's my nose?"

376 nurture baby dolls

Children often enjoy learning to nurture babies. Toddlers especially love to take care of someone who's younger than they are, an activity that helps them develop empathy. Tending to dolls or plush toys serves a similar function—and they're fun to cuddle.

377 make a shallow lake

Use a hose to make a puddle of water in a small tarp spread over grass. Add plastic animals, boats, and dolls, and watch your child as he rules (and wades around and sits in) his watery kingdom. Always supervise him carefully—never leave him to rule alone.

378 watch planes soar

Airplanes fascinate toddlers: after all, they're huge and they fly! Find a good viewing point (a park near an airport is ideal) and encourage your child to study the planes as they pass overhead. Stretch her imagination by talking about where the planes might be going.

379 love a ladybug

Look for ladybugs outside, or make your own by drawing black spots on red construction-paper circles and coloring in a black area for the head. Explain that they're good for gardens because they eat the bugs that eat our plants. They don't bite us, though they may pinch lightly with their tiny jaws. Let your child sniff one. Yuck! Ladybugs don't smell good, but they're awfully good for our gardens.

382 hit the hardware store

What's better than a Saturday morning outing to the hardware store? The scent of freshly cut lumber, the dazzle of brilliantly colored paint samples, the feel of scratchy sandpaper. To adults and toddlers alike, a hardware store offers up dozens of sensory possibilities.

12+ months

380 croon a lullaby

Not every song has to have a bouncing rhyme or a fingerplay. A soft lullaby is perfect for times when your child is snuggled close to you, almost asleep.

381 get up and at 'em

Cruising around your furniture is a great way for your little one to get mobile. He will particularly like soft things, like cushions to climb on and over, making his very own obstacle course to flex his motor skills.

384 hang out in a hammock

On a sunny day—even a chilly one if you're armed with a cozy blanket—it's great to snuggle with your toddler in a hammock. For a little downtime, cuddle up and rock gently while you read a story together, talk, or just watch the tree branches swaying overhead.

385 throw things

Don't let toddler experiments with gravity (otherwise known as throwing food from the highchair) get you down. You might want to discourage that particular activity by ignoring it, then rechannel his curiosity by taking him outside to observe how different things behave when he drops or tosses them. Cookies, rocks, feathers, and bubbles all move through the air a little differently—and every bit of that data will be filed away in your budding scientist's busy brain.

383 browse a bookstore

Whether you pop in to check out the latest titles or come for kids' storytime or a reading by a children's book author, bookstores offer lots of opportunities for fun and learning. Even if you don't manage to get out of there without some new storybooks, a bookstore visit is still relatively inexpensive and makes for long-lasting, valuable toddler entertainment.

386 bag some toys

Hang a shoe bag—the kind designed to hang on the back of a door—at your child's level. Invite him to make a sorting game of putting away small plush toys in the pockets. Line them up by type (for instance, all the cats or bears), size, or color.

387 mouse around

This song is a fun way to expose your child to the concepts of numbers and counting. Make up extra verses to rhyme with the strike number, such as "The clock struck two, the mouse kissed you."
Hickory dickory dock.
clap your hands three times
The mouse ran up the clock.
run your fingers up your child's left arm
The clock struck one,
clap once over your child's head
The mouse ran down,
run your fingers down your child's right arm
Hickory dickory dock!
clap your hands three times

388 be a massage therapist

To give your child a calming massage, undress her down to her diaper and lay her on her tummy on a soft towel on the floor. Warm a dab of baby lotion between your hands, then stroke her back from shoulders to hips. Although all toddlers are different, many prefer a firm but gentle hand—not at all rough, but not too tickly and light. Move on to her arms and legs. Is she still awake? Repeat the process on the front of her body, too.

389 carry crayons

Time spent waiting for the pediatrician in the exam room might feel long and nerve-racking for your toddler. But you can turn it into a time to play with a box of crayons. Why do you think that lovely long sheet of paper is there on the exam table?

390 place a puzzle piece

The first time your child does a puzzle, give him just one piece to fit. As his spatial sense improves over time, give him more and more pieces, until he can do the whole puzzle.

391 test while you play

Play games that help you track your toddler's visual development and hearing. Move toys back and forth and in and out of her field of vision, watching her eyes to see whether they follow the toy. To test hearing, lower your voice and whisper something—make sure she seems to hear and understand you. If your child's responses seem off to you, discuss them with your doctor.

 tip *Reading stories, rhymes, and poems increases your child's vocabulary and shares your love of books.*

392 nip biting in the bud

Teething pain, the lack of an appropriate verbal way to express strong emotions, or even sheer joy can lead your toddler to sink his teeth into the world. Read an age-appropriate book about biting together to help explain why biting isn't an acceptable outlet for these emotions. If your child bites, gently take him to a quiet spot. When he's calmer, explain that biting just isn't OK—ever.

393 chill out

Your toddler needs a little "me" time now and again. So let her spend a few quiet minutes on a special blanket on the floor to give her a quick break from her busy day and to let her practice amusing herself.

394 recall the animals

After an excursion to a farm, petting zoo, or a pet store, ask your toddler to name the animals he saw. Sing "Old MacDonald" and include the animals he met that day.

395 build a nest

Too cold or rainy for your little one to play outside? Gather up all the cushions you can find and, since you're the big bird, build a nest for her in a quiet corner. Add a few plush toys (especially if you have toy birds!) and a little cup of birdseed (cereal or small crackers). Try this in the middle of the afternoon and be ready with a soft blanket so you can tuck in your little bird for a nap in her nest.

396 master peekaboo

When your toddler is about a year old, he can understand that you'll still be there when you cover your face with your hands. He continues to love peekaboo, though, probably because he's old enough now to be in control—he may even initiate the game himself. Make it slightly more sophisticated by varying the way you play: peek around corners or over and under your newspaper.

397 pinch cereal

Encourage your child to practice her growing control of her own hands and fingers, especially her pincer grip. Put a small handful of dry cereal in a bowl and demonstrate picking up the cereal pieces, one by one, and dropping them into a second bowl. Then let her have a try.

398 sing a soggy song

This song is perfect for a rainy day.
It's raining, it's pouring,
The old man is snoring.
He went to bed and bumped his head
And couldn't get up in the morning.
Rain, rain, go away
Come again another day.
Little (your child's name)
wants to play!

399 build a kiddie library

Books on shelves can be tough to retrieve, so a big basket on the floor makes an excellent toddler library. As your child's storybooks multiply, rotate them so he doesn't get bored or overwhelmed (but don't put away all of his favorite books at once).

400 get rolling

Outfit your child with a low shopping cart with a high handle—just right for her to grasp as she pushes it. Such a cart provides stability for walking and, with a little imagination, almost unlimited play value. Today, it's a car; next week, a nest for a toy chicken and a plastic egg; next month, a garden cart for hauling sticks around the yard.

12+ months

401 have a rug toss

Throwing is easier than catching at first, and a small beanbag animal or a rolled-up scarf can be easier to handle than a ball. Bring out a few of them and a small rug or a bath mat. Ask your child to stand close to the rug and try throwing the animal or scarf onto it. Then gradually move the rug a bit farther away and help him build his gross motor skills.

402 read together

Promote your child's love of reading by example. Have family reading times when everyone grabs a book and settles in. Your toddler can join a family member or look at a picture book on her own. Never leave home without a book to read together in case you have to wait somewhere. In time, she'll come to see books and reading as one of life's great—and reliable—pleasures.

403 ease him in

Everyone enjoys a happy child, but sometimes the attention of friendly strangers will be too much for your toddler, especially in new situations or places. Stay close to him and ask him if he would like to say "hello" or wave "good-bye." Giving him choices helps him feel in control.

404 hammer it out

Hammering is terrific fun for your toddler, and it develops fine motor control and eye-hand coordination. Look for toy tool sets or pounding toys that she can use with your close supervision.

405 paint footprints

Unroll large sheets of paper on a washable surface (like the kitchen floor) and put a few colors of nontoxic liquid paint out on paper plates. Let your toddler step in the paint with bare feet, and hold his hands while he "paints" his footprints all over the paper. Then hang his creation in his room, or use it for wrapping gifts.

406 free the feet

Until your child is walking on her own out of doors, she doesn't need real shoes (nonslip socks or booties will keep her tootsies warm). When she goes barefoot in the grass, make sure the area is free of sharp stones, sticks, stinging insects, and litter. And check the sand at the beach—it can be hot enough to burn on a summer day. But as long as you're careful, you and your toddler can enjoy the barefooted pleasure of swishing through soft grass, padding along the water's edge at the beach, or squishing through mud after a rainstorm.

407 read the signals

If your child turns away, pushes his hands out at you, or puts his fist up by his ear, it might mean, "Just give me a moment, OK?" But if he's raising his arms, grinning, or bouncing excitedly, he's raring to go. Practice reading his signals—and explain your own while you're at it so that he can learn to read them, too.

408 trot out a knee ride

Seat your toddler on your knees, facing you, and hold her hands as you "trot" your knees in time to this horsey rhyme:
Trot, little pony,
Trot to town.
Trot, little pony,
Don't fall dowwwnnn!

409 get messy

Sometimes it's good to be messy. Your little one will love using nontoxic fingerpaints and may also revel in playing with his food or digging in the dirt. This is all good fun, but he may also enjoy getting clean again.

410 have a ball ...or three

One ball is great, but a few of different sizes are even better. For kids who have mastered standing, kicking comes next. A soft rubber ball or beach ball about 10 inches (25 cm) in diameter is perfect for kicking. Smaller balls are good for dropping and rolling, but be sure they're large enough so that they don't present a choking hazard.

411 follow the string trail

Kids love to explore, especially when there's treasure at the end of the journey. Using a brightly colored ball of yarn, wind a trail through your house. Supervising carefully, help your child follow the trail as it runs from his bedroom door, down the hall, loops around the corner into the living room, then winds in and out among the dining room chairs until he comes to the yarn's end, hidden in a box or bag containing a small treat. If he gathers up yarn as he goes, the path will be easier to follow.

412 try out new hairdos

Hang an unbreakable mirror on the wall behind the faucet in the bathtub. To make washing more fun, use the suds from tear-free shampoo to sculpt hairdo shapes. Get creative with waves, cone-shaped spirals—and maybe even horns or a beard and mustache.

413 refine your bedtime ritual

As your baby transforms into a toddler, it's a good time to evaluate her bedtime routine. Does she need more time to talk or cuddle as she winds down from her busy day? Should you be reading longer books or picking out a new CD to listen to? Perhaps you could even sing a soft song together.

414 make an indoor sandbox

Set a plastic dishpan on a tray and empty a large box of oatmeal into it. Give your toddler cups and spoons for pouring and digging, plastic horses for grazing, or toy cars and trucks for tunneling through the oats.

 tip *Tactile play is fun. Let your little one explore different textures, such as sand, flour, and modeling clay.*

415 talk to the animals

Gather up some plush animals and arrange them in a circle around your child. Ask him to make each animal's special sound, then call on each one as if in a classroom: "Dog, you're next—a dog says … ?"

417 choose some mood music

Pick different music to listen to according to your and your toddler's activities and moods. Be sure, though, that you enjoy times when the background noises are turned off and your child can hear herself think and listen to the natural sounds of her world. Give her the gift of learning to appreciate silence.

12+ months

416 sing a song of fingers

Here's a great song for naming each finger.
"Where is Thumbkin, where is Thumbkin?"
raise your hands as if asking a question
"Here I am, here I am."
wiggle your left thumb, then wiggle your right thumb
"How are you today, sir?" "Very well, I thank you."
make your thumbs "bow" and "nod"
"Run away, run away."
hide both your hands behind your back, then bring each finger out in turn and repeat with:
Where is pointer? Where is middle finger? Where is ring finger? and *Where is pinkie?*

418 pretend to wash up

Here's a wishy-washy fingerplay just for fun.
Wash the dishes,
wipe your hand in a circular motion one way
Wipe the dishes,
and back the other way
Ring the bell for tea.
mime ringing a bell
Three good kisses,
kiss your child on each of his cheeks and on his nose
Three good wishes,
tap gently three times on his forehead
I will give to thee.
point to yourself and then to your child

18+

eighteen months & up

milestones

Your toddler is listening more attentively to conversations going on around her.

- She is also becoming more assertive and clearly lets you know what she wants

- Learning to successfully use a spoon to feed herself builds her independence and self-esteem.

- When she looks in a mirror, she is beginning to recognize herself and understand that she is a unique being.

Your toddler's expanding vocabulary of a dozen or so words and budding ability to form two- and three-word phrases make real conversations possible and often lead to a riotous exploration of humor. Increasingly nimble fingers help her build block castles, throw balls, and scribble art. Her increased mobility sometimes has the reverse effect of making her clingy. She wants to try and do everything herself but still wants you to be nearby.

18+ months

419 have high tea

Your toddler's improving language skills and growing imagination might lead to more involved pretend play, such as a delightfully elaborate tea party. You can use a toy teapot to help her pour "tea" into the cups of her "guests," and serve cookies or fruit. This isn't only pretend play—it's also great practice for future social occasions.

420 mind strangers

Your child will pick up on your level of comfort with strangers. Keep him close by when you're out and about, and he will follow your lead on the people who make you feel comfortable as well as those who don't. When possible, talk ahead of time about who you might meet.

421 pause for a poem

Your toddler will love the dramatic tension if you both pause for a second after the number "four" when you recite this poem.
The clock stands still
stand up straight and tall
While the hands move around.
move your arms around like the hands on a clock
One o'clock, two o'clock, three o'clock, four—
clap your hands with each number
Round and round, now touch the floor!
turn around on the spot and touch the floor
Cuckoo!

422 let your bookworm "read"

With you toddler's increased mobility and "busyness," he may have trouble sitting still during storytime. One solution is to hold him in your lap and ask him to read to you. "What do you see here?" you can ask. "That's right—a billy goat! What's the goat doing? What do you think he'll do next?" Let him decide when it's time to turn to a new page.

423 get that rhythm

Reading to your toddler is about more than the words you speak or the pictures he sees on the page. Help him with language skills now and reading skills down the road by bouncing him gently to keep time with the words, emphasizing the language's rhythm by repeating words that sound good together, or tapping out the syllables on your child's arm.

424 fill some big shoes

Challenge balance, encourage imitative play, and have a laugh: let your toddler take a walk in Mommy's or Daddy's shoes, literally.

425 get creative with cups

One of the best—and least expensive—toy purchases you'll ever make is a set of stacking plastic cups. Besides basic stacking, they're great for molding sand castles, washing a doll's hair, holding a "lake" for tiny boats to float in, tracing circles, learning about sizes—you name it. Just hand a set to your toddler and watch what he does with them.

426 pack a travel tote

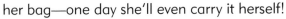

Stock a small tote bag with crayons, paper, a plush toy, a sock puppet, a book, a drink, and a snack for your toddler. This portable entertainment kit is great for long drives or tiresome lines. Make sure she knows it's her bag—one day she'll even carry it herself!

18+ months

427 whip up some jellies

It's a snack! It's a toy! It's jellies!
4 packets unflavored gelatin
2 cups cold fruit juice, such as apple or grape
2 cups hot fruit juice, heated until just boiling
The parent part: Pour the cold juice into a large heatproof bowl. Sprinkle the gelatin over the cold juice and let stand for 1 minute. Add the hot juice and stir gently but thoroughly until the gelatin dissolves. Pour into an ungreased 9 x 13-inch (23 x 33 cm) cake pan and refrigerate until set.
The toddler or parent part: Use cookie cutters (simple shapes work best for small hands) to cut out the jellies. Or just use a knife (definitely a grown-up job!) to cut the whole sheet into squares.
The toddler part: Poke the jellies with your finger. Stack them up and watch them shimmy. Bounce them. Oh, and eat them, too!

 tip *Talk about textures with your toddler. It will help him understand objects in a three-dimensional way.*

428 make an animal farm

When is a shoe box not a shoe box? When it's a barn! Cover a box with red construction paper, cut out double barn doors and windows, and set it on green construction paper. Add a silo made from an oatmeal box, plastic farm animals, and a sprinkling of shredded-wheat "hay" for a complete farm experience.

429 lessen life's stings

After your child takes a tumble, get down on the same level by sitting beside him or holding him in your lap. Acknowledge his pain ("That looks like it hurt!"), but don't fuss over minor accidents. With a scrape or cut, minimize the sight of blood by using a dark-colored washcloth. When he's getting an injection, have him blow out as hard as he can while he's getting the shot. With a more serious medical event, such as a painful ear infection, be his advocate and ask a doctor for the best way to relieve his pain. Studies show that healing is faster when pain is controlled.

430 feel good

Collect small pieces of cloth and paper of different textures: velvet, sandpaper, cellophane, burlap, silk, tissue. Sit with your child and feel them together, one by one. "This one is smooth, isn't it? Does the sandpaper feel smooth, too? What about the furry one? It feels soft, doesn't it?" This stimulates her sense of touch and increases her vocabulary.

431 play in the sand

For sandbox or sand-table play, give your child a variety of cups, funnels, empty spice jars with shaker lids, and colanders. Add water and supervise carefully as you let her explore all of sand's tactile possibilities by pouring, shaking, and shaping her "sandscape."

432 paint a "watercolor"

Let your toddler "paint" the outside of the house (or the deck, the sidewalk, or the fence) with a bucket of water and a big paintbrush. Talk about how the water changes the color of whatever she's painting. She can cool off by painting herself, too—but always supervise any water play.

433 splash up a storm

Fill the kitchen sink with warm soapy water and throw in some plastic cups and bottles. While you're right beside her, let your child stand on a chair (with its back to the counter for greater stability) and play in the sink as long as you're willing to stand there (don't leave her unattended though, not even for a moment).

436 sort it out together

Get your child thinking about how things are grouped into categories by having her help you sort clean laundry. Have her find all the socks or all the shirts and place them in a basket for you to fold.

434 outfit your handyperson

Equip your child with authentic versions of grown-up tools and equipment. Real but miniature garden tools, small brooms, and plastic hammers and screwdrivers will help kids make themselves useful around the house. And toddlers love to feel like they're making a contribution!

435 let him cling

On some days your toddler will be a brave, bold, and fearless explorer; on other days he will be your little shadow, following you around and clinging on to you for reassurance and affectionate hugs. Talk about his fears and role-play scary situations.

437 do the wash

Toddlers love to imitate what you do, enjoy cleaning up, and are thrilled with water play. Combine all three by letting your child set up a toy laundry to wash his doll blankets, toy monkey's shirt, and plush puppy's ribbon collar. Give him a pan of warm water with just a tiny bit of soap, and another pan of plain water for rinsing. (Make sure you stay close by to supervise.) Improvise a clothesline, let him lay the items on a towel to dry, or help him pop them into the dryer.

438 hit the beach

A beach is 360 degrees of pure surround sound—and surround smells, sights, textures, and even tastes (salt water!). Protect your child with sunscreen, a T-shirt, and a floppy hat, then let him explore, always with your supervision. Pouring, digging, and piling sand; feeling the water on his feet while you hold his hand—all are great ways to expand his sensory horizons.

439 issue a command

Now that your toddler knows more words and has a better memory, following commands can become a game. If processing one task is easy, challenge him with more complex instructions, such as, "Put the book on the table and the teddy bear on the couch."

440 play with food

Use a nontoxic marker to draw a trail of large dots on a piece of construction paper, and put out a bowl of oyster crackers. See if your child can place one cracker on each dot. As his fine motor control improves over time, use smaller foods such as dry cereal pieces.

 tip *Grasping and releasing objects builds the fine motor skills needed for drawing and, eventually, writing.*

441 jingle bells

Securely stitch large bells to circles of waistband elastic that are big enough to slip onto your child's ankles and wrists. Join him in some dancing and clapping so they jingle and jangle. Make sure you are always around to supervise his play with these bells.

442 teach the bare necessities

Taking clothes off is often much more fun than putting them on at this stage. Being naked is great in the right context—so help her feel comfortable—but also explain that clothes are expected in most places. Going bare in the backyard now and then can make up for having to keep her pants on at the park!

443 make a bird snack

Encourage a love of animals by asking your child to assist you when you go out to refill the bird feeders and birdbath. To make a crunchy bird snack, invite her to help you smear a pinecone with nut butter, then roll it in birdseed.

444 hail to the chef!

Your toddler will be delighted when you ask him to perform kitchen duty. He can carry his unbreakable cup to the sink, put a clean towel away in a drawer, or place rolls in a basket on the table. This is a great time to get him used to the concept that everyone can find a way to participate and lend a hand. He's also probably getting quite good at opening things, though, so be certain to keep all materials that might cause injury securely locked up or well out of reach.

445 dabble with paint

Cut pieces of string into different lengths, up to about 10 inches (25 cm), and dab them in pools of nontoxic liquid paint poured out on paper plates. Help your toddler drag the paint-covered strings across white or colored paper to create abstract designs.

nut butter

446 blow some bubble art

Stir some nontoxic liquid paint into a little bubble-blowing solution, and show your toddler how to blow a storm of colored bubbles onto a large piece of paper. Voilà—instant soap art!

447 recount the day

Talk with your child about her adventures at the end of each day. It helps her exercise her memory—and it also helps her to unwind. Ask a few questions to help her along.

448 bond with some bugs

Lie facedown on the grass with your toddler and put an embroidery hoop or a loop of string on the ground in front of you. How many different creatures can you see inside this little universe? Are they eating? Working? Just hanging out? Those activities sound like the sort of things you and your toddler enjoy!

449 cook up a menu

Make a restaurant menu for home, with pictures of a few favorite healthy foods cut from a magazine. Present it to your toddler with a flourish at mealtime, asking, "What will you have today, madam?" Being allowed to choose boosts her sense of independence, but the menu's limited options help avoid frustration.

450 stick on safety decals

Putting themed large stickers on sliding glass doors at your child's eye level serves a dual purpose: it will help him see the glass door, and studying and talking about the decals together will build his vocabulary.

451 toot a kazoo

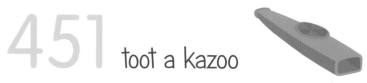

If your toddler can hum, she can also make music with a kazoo. She won't just broaden her musical experience; she'll also produce some great sound effects: silly voices get sillier, race cars become vroomier, and ducks are quackier with a kazoo.

tip *Your toddler's sense of humor is starting to emerge, and she will revel in the chance to make you laugh.*

452 hide and peek

While your child watches, hide two small toys in the room, and ask him to find them. Slowly increase the number of objects to keep the game challenging, but stop while he's still successful and having fun.

453 encourage independence

Toddlers prize their increasing independence. If your child wants to pick out her own clothes, narrow the choices: "Which will it be, the blue shirt or the white?" If she wants to pour milk on her cereal, give her some in a cup, not the whole carton. Let her make some decisions: "We need to go to the library and the post office. Which do you want to do first?"

454 shake a tambourine

Two paper plates and a handful of dry cereal make a terrific tambourine. Give your child some crayons to decorate the bottoms of the plates. Then, with the cereal on one plate, use nontoxic glue to join the plates together, making sure the decorated sides face out. Secure by punching holes around the edge and lacing the plates together using a long ribbon. Now put on some music and get shakin'.

455 hop on a bus

If you and your family go most places in the car, take a short trip with your toddler using a different mode of transportation. If you're city dwellers, ride a bus to a destination a few stops away or take the subway to the park. If you live outside the city, you might ride a commuter train into town or cross a river on a ferry. Supervise your child closely; hitting the road is fun but requires extra caution.

456 share smooches

Kissing takes coordination. When your toddler returns a kiss, it means things are coming together for him: lip control, trust, turn taking, and the ability to express his feelings.

457 avoid foul balls

Keep the ball from rolling off course by sitting across from your toddler with your legs open and his feet against the inside of your legs. Roll the ball back and forth inside the enclosed diamond formed by your legs.

458 let your garden grow

Good garden help isn't so hard to find after all. Young yard workers can pick up sticks, drop seeds into holes in the soil, and water (under your supervision) with a watering can.

459 stack 'em high

Your child has probably graduated to stacking or arranging about six to eight blocks by this stage. Help hone his architectural prowess—and his understanding of size, shape, and balance—by sitting down with him to build something a little bit more elaborate together, say, a castle or a skyscraper.

460 create a land of cushions

Help your child build a place of her own out of all the sofa and chair cushions you can round up. Stand them on end for walls, stack them for towers or thrones, and strew them around the floor for magic stepping-stones. If the walls come tumbling down? No harm done—just stand them up again or build something new and even more fanciful.

461 welcome book choices

Encourage your child to look at books alone and to pick out ones you'll read together. You'll be surprised by how often his preferences change.

462 explore the library

Your child can get a lot out of a trip to the library long before she's reading, so visit one regularly. You might ask about scheduled storytimes and activities for toddlers, or just go to take a look at the books. Some libraries schedule short movies, picnics, or playgroups. The concept of borrowing a book and giving it back the next week is hard to grasp at first, but soon she'll be eager for "library day" so she can trade in last week's treasures for new ones.

463 "print out" a rainbow

Draw an outline of a rainbow on paper. Mix small amounts of nontoxic liquid paint, and have your child fill the rainbow with her colorful fingerprints.

466 arrange play dates

Other children around the same age fascinate toddlers, and they will happily play alongside each other (called "parallel play"). When your little one is playing with other kids, though, stay close by to help him take turns with his toys and treat his playmate the way that he likes to be treated.

464 feel with feet

Give your toddler a few large plastic tubs of squishy, sandy, and gooey substances like mud, sand, and jelly. Watch her explore the world—with her feet.

465 be her support

A toddler is acutely sensitive to her parents' reactions, so it's vital not to scold or tease her when she falters in confidence or gets scared. Prepare her for potentially tough situations by discussing them ahead of time. Then move on together to an activity you know she can do well.

468 take a toy inventory

Include in your child's toy box a variety of toys that encourage developmental skills: blocks for fine motor skills; push toys for gross motor skills; materials for making or listening to music; lots of age-appropriate books; dolls and plush animals to encourage nurturing instincts; and playthings such as cars, kitchen items, and dress-up clothes to promote imitative and imaginative play.

467 greet another jack and jill

Is it a fingerplay—or a wingding?
Two little blackbirds sitting on a hill,
bounce your index fingers in front of you
One named Jack
wiggle one of your index fingers
And one named Jill.
wiggle your other index finger
Fly away, Jack.
turn one of your hands into a "wing" and flap away, hiding your hand behind you
Fly away, Jill.
do the same with your other hand
Come back, Jack! Come back, Jill!
bring your "birds" back one at a time

469 walk and talk

As you're walking with your child through your neighborhood, tease his imagination and get him thinking about the people in his surroundings. Stop outside a house and talk with him about what might be going on inside: "I see a stroller. Do you think a baby lives there? And there's a leash on the porch—they must have a puppy!"

470 adorn a book bag

Buy a plain sturdy canvas bag and transform it into your child's personal book bag. Use nontoxic liquid paint to help her adorn it with her handprints or with stamps made with apples that have been cut in half and dipped in the paint. Then use a fabric marker to add her name.

471 cook a pizza

Take a softball-sized piece of store-bought or basic homemade bread dough and pull off about a quarter of that piece. Form the first, larger piece into a flat circle—the turtle's shell—about 4 to 6 inches (10 to 15 cm) across. Divide the smaller piece into six pieces. Use the small pieces to shape an oval turtle head, four legs, and a tail, and press them into their proper places on the dough. Spread marinara sauce on the turtle's shell, and have your child decorate it with shredded cheese, pepperoni slices, olives, or other toppings. Press two little olive bits into the turtle's head for eyes. Make a turtle pizza for everyone, letting family members choose their own toppings. Bake in a preheated 450°F (230°C) oven for 6 to 10 minutes, watching carefully to make sure your turtles don't burn.

472 make a lantern

Have your child decorate a piece of paper with nontoxic markers or crayons. With her artwork on the outside, fold the paper in half crosswise, and then cut 3-inch (7.5 cm) slits at regular intervals along the creased edge. Unfold and curl lengthwise into a loose tube. Fasten edges with nontoxic glue, stand the tube up, and admire her fine paper lantern.

473 think inside the box

Toddlers this age love big boxes to play in, but don't expect complex imaginative play yet. Your child may not be ready to rocket to the moon in the box the television came in, but she'll relish the cozy space, the flaps to open and close, or maybe the chance to hide away for a nap with a blanket.

474 draw different strokes

By the middle of his second year, your child probably can hold a crayon (the chunky kind is easier for little hands to grasp) and even make deliberate strokes on a piece of paper. Demonstrate drawing a horizontal line, and ask him to try following your example. Then do the same with a vertical line. If he's enjoying imitating your drawing, move on to a cross. Then let him cut loose and scribble.

 tip *If he tries out his artistry on the walls, warming crayon marks with a hair dryer makes them easier to wipe off.*

475 row that boat

Exercise your child's motor skills and balance by having him "row" with a plush toy seated in his lap.

Row, row, row your boat
Gently down the stream
Merrily, merrily, merrily, merrily,
Life is but a dream.

18+
months

476 let those feelings out

Sometimes a day away from you may end with a meltdown. Even if your toddler had a great time, he may be tired and ready to release the strong feelings that built up during the day. And who better to share those feelings with than you, the person he feels safest with? So if he needs to release a little steam, let him.

477 tell it to the hand

Don a sock puppet and use it to ask your child questions about her life and daily activities. She may share some novel insights with her funny new friend.

478 do some target practice

Roll down the top edges of three paper grocery bags to make a short, a medium, and a tall basket for throwing practice. Give your child some soft objects like sponges, and ask her to aim at the shortest and closest basket first, then move on to the taller targets farther away.

479 create new sounds

Collect three plastic containers, such as yogurt cups. Fill one with large buttons, one with large bells, and one with marshmallows. Tape the tops securely, then ask your child to shake each one. Watch him enjoy the sounds he creates.

480 make a "quiet kit"

Place an activity basket near the phone to buy a few minutes of quiet when you have to make or take an important call. Include toys that aren't noisy, a small flashlight, and some sock puppets that only whisper.

481 picture this

Put together a photo album of relatives and friends for your toddler. Look at it together and talk about the people you see: "Who's that? That's right, it's Aunt Kris—she's Molly's mommy." This type of album is especially good for kids with long-distance relatives.

482 save the bunny

This fingerplay appeals to kids' nurturing instincts.
In a cabin in the woods,
a small child by the window stood,
touch your fingers together to make a roof over your head; use your index finger to draw the square window
Saw a rabbit hopping near, knocking at the door.
making a peace sign for the rabbit's ears, "hop" your hand in front of you
"Help me, help me," the rabbit cried,
"I just need a place to hide."
throw your arms up twice in alarm
"Come little rabbit, come inside,
wave your hand toward you to beckon the rabbit
I'll take care of you."
cradle an imaginary rabbit
in your arms

483 recite a rhyme

Holding your child on your lap, bounce to this rhyme to teach the feel of language:
Intery, mintery, cattery corn,
Apple seed and apple thorn.
Wire, briar, limber lock,
Five geese in a flock.
Sit and sing by the spring,
O-U-T! And in again.
lower your child between your knees

18+ months

484 zip, snap, button!

At 18 months your toddler is developing the fine motor control and self-care skills to help dress himself. Find a book or doll that lets him practice with buttons, zippers, and other closures. Clothes that have roomy necks, big buttons, and zippers with large pull tabs help at this "I did it myself!" stage.

485 point out initials

Toward the middle of your child's second year, start pointing out her name in print. Emphasize her first initial and talk about other words that share the same initial sound. "Dog starts the same way your name does—listen: d-d-d-dog, D-D-D-Dana!"

486 give kitty a thrill

Dim the lights and let your toddler provide a flashlight "mouse" for a cat to chase. This is a great way for a young child who might be a little nervous about touching a cat to interact with him. Besides, playing with a flashlight is always fun!

487 enjoy nature in the city

Can't make it to the wilderness this weekend? A trip to a garden center is free entertainment, though it may be hard to resist bringing home some little green friends. Supervise closely as your toddler wanders through a forest of plants. When you're only a few feet tall, a display of fountains and birdbaths looks like a pint-sized lake district, a tray of cacti is a strange no-petting zoo, and a leafy, misty greenhouse becomes an Amazon rain forest.

488 play favorites

There are times when only Mommy will do. Or only Daddy. Or only the babysitter. Don't be offended if your child plays favorites. She's getting to know the people in her life and learning to appreciate their different styles. It won't take her long to figure out that Grandpa swings her just right, or that Aunt Maria does the best monkey imitation. When you're the favorite, just do what you do best.

489 color in the snow

Tint water with dark food coloring and help your child use it in well-rinsed squirt bottles to "draw" on the snow or to "clothe" a snowman. He can also decorate snow figures with ice "jewels"—colored water that's been frozen in ice-cube trays.

492 dance ring-around-the-rosy

Show a gang of kids how to walk in a circle (hand-holding optional) and collapse at the appropriate time. Or grasp your child's hands and dance around in a circle for just two: *Ring around the rosy, pocket full of posies. Ashes, ashes, we all fall DOWN!*

490 take turns hiding

As your toddler becomes more adept at playing hide-and-seek, teach him to hide. He'll mostly hide his head, not realizing that his legs or fingers are sticking out. But be sure to act surprised when you do find him.

491 blow a tune

Make a nifty instrument using a wide cardboard tube covered at one end with a piece of wax paper. Humming into the tube (like sucking from a straw or blowing out candles) helps strengthen the muscles that your child uses to speak. Plus, your toddler will love the new noise!

18+
months

493 dig some dinosaurs

Why do tiny people love enormous animals? Maybe because in their budding imaginations they're starting to see themselves as larger, more powerful creatures. Your child may love dinosaur toys, and, as he gets older—and better at longer outings—he might enjoy dinosaur events at museums, too.

494 do some milky magic

Pour milk into a shallow round bowl. Have your child watch as you carefully—without stirring—drop four drops of food coloring randomly onto the surface of the milk. Then add a drop of liquid dishwashing soap in the center of the bowl, and voilà, it's tie-dyed (but not drinkable!) milk.

495 reassure your trouper

Your child's fears can be fickle: one day the neighbor's dog and the giant model of a lobster are funny; the next, they're downright creepy. Don't make a big deal out of these fears. Just let your child know that he's safe—and that you're there to look out for him.

496 make edible art

Finger paint with instant pudding. Strip your little one down to her diaper and give her some big sheets of paper and a plastic bowl of pudding so she can make some sweet artwork.

 tip *Give your budding artist lots of encouragement and freedom to express herself in her own unique way.*

497 jazz up a shirt

Cut the root end off a bunch of celery and help your child use it as a stamp to decorate a T-shirt. Dab the celery "stamp" in nontoxic paint and, with a sheet of cardboard inside the shirt to keep the design from bleeding through, stamp away. Once the shirt's dry, run it through a warm dryer for 20 minutes to make the design last longer.

498 sing the abc's

Sometimes it's good to let learning creep up on your little one. Sing the alphabet song as a knee-bouncing rhyme, a lullaby, a jazz song, or even a pop jingle. In two or three years when he's learning to read, he'll realize that he already knows the alphabet.

499 separate gently

The parenting books said your toddler would go through separation anxiety at nine months, and chances are she did. But she'll still have days when she clings, so respect her feelings and allow extra transition time when you need to leave.

500 spot him

Try out this activity to get a better sense of how your toddler sees himself and his world. Without him knowing what you're doing, sneak a dot of lipstick or face paint on his cheek or forehead, then put him in front of a mirror. Does he point at the spot on his image in the mirror or reach up to his own face? Sometime around the middle of your toddler's second year, he'll switch from pointing to the spot in the mirror to raising his hand to touch his forehead. Once this happens, you know your little one has begun to develop a sense that he's "me," his own person, separate from everyone else.

18+ months

501 check out the playground

A playground boasts more play equipment than you have room for in your yard, and often has a child-safe material underfoot to make falls less likely to cause injury. For a child this age attractions such as hiding places to look out of, low surfaces and inclines to climb over, and sandboxes to dig in are great.

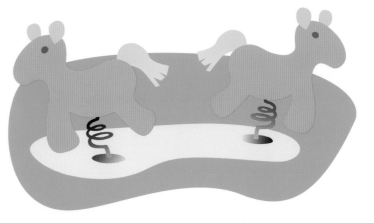

24+ twenty-four months & up

milestones

Look for explosive growth in your toddler's ability to understand and use words.

• Participating in more involved conversations helps her exercise language and social skills.

• Watch as she starts to enjoy playing interactively with peers and learning about sharing.

• Encourage her to follow simple sequences of instructions; succeeding at tasks big and small builds self-esteem.

Your two-year-old's personality is clearly blossoming a bit each day. She isn't shy about sharing her opinions and is quick to respond with an automatic "no" to assert her growing independence. However, you are still the lens through which your child sees the universe; your ways of interacting with the world help to shape hers. The big task for your toddler is to learn about herself—what she likes and how she can participate in the world more fully.

502 pamper your pets

It's not too early to involve your toddler in the care of family pets. A two-year-old can pour a cup of kibble into the dog's bowl. Teach patience and gentleness, but keep your child safe by instructing him never to bother an animal that's eating or sleeping—and by supervising all close encounters of the furry kind. Don't overreact if a provoked cat scratches or a dog nips lightly—if you do, the child may become fearful. Say something like, "Ooh, Tux got scared when he felt his tail being pulled—let's pet him gently on the back and go put something on that scratch."

503 seek out shapes

Play a game to hone your child's ability to recognize shapes. Start with an easy one on a picture-book page ("Can you find something shaped like a circle?") and graduate to finding circles, squares, and other shapes out in the real world. "How about that flower box? That's right, it's a rectangle. What about the moon?"

504 turn negative positive

Your child's favorite word at this stage might be "no"—an outgrowth of her increasing sense of self and desire to shape her world. Let her assert the power of "no" by asking absurd questions like "Are we standing in the ocean?" so she can respond with a resounding "No!"

505 dress up and pretend

Add four or five pieces of fabric, in a range of textures and colors, to your child's toy chest. They should be the right size to make a bullfighter's cloak, a butterfly's wings, a picnic cloth, or a plush animal's blanket. You'll be amazed at all the dress-up and pretend-play uses he'll find for these simple bits of fabric.

506 encourage reading

When your child begins pretending to read—or babbling as she follows the words—she has reached a great milestone in preliteracy. Even knowing how to turn pages in the right direction is an important skill. Encourage her literary interest by storing her favorite books within her reach in a basket on the floor or on a low shelf. Now you can take turns reading to each other.

507 shake some maracas

Help your child make maracas by dropping dried beans, lentils, or unpopped popcorn into a small plastic water bottle. Glue or tape the lid in place securely and watch as your child plays to make sure the lid doesn't come loose, as small items can be dangerous if they find their way into small mouths.

508 follow a pattern

Build on your child's growing understanding of patterns by getting ambitious with bead stringing. Using large wooden beads or spools, suggest an easy pattern like round-square-round-square. Or help him to put different colors in order—for example, green-blue-green.

509 sniff it out

The nose knows, so ask your child to close her eyes, then stimulate her senses by asking her to sniff and identify safe kitchen items. Vanilla, cinnamon, and cocoa are good ones to start with. Avoid peppers or spicy things that might irritate her nose or eyes.

510 get handy

Coat your child's hands with nontoxic liquid paint and ask him to press them on a sheet of paper. Handprints make great designs, and you can even encourage him to experiment with different colored paints. You don't necessarily need to let the paint dry between passes; if the picture is still wet, he'll delight in mixing hues to create a rainbow of vivid prints. And once the paint has finally dried, he can add details with nontoxic crayons. Add your own handprints, too!

511 work a wagon

While you're working in the yard, give your child a series of small pickup and delivery jobs to accomplish with her wagon. For instance, you might say, "Pile up all the leaves you can in your wagon and take them to the trash can, please."

 tip *Give your toddler small tasks to help you. This encourages empathy and helps her learn new skills.*

512 wash the dog

If your dog is well behaved, letting your child help you wash her can be a riot—and everyone gets a bath! Have on hand one dog, one toddler, the garden hose, dog shampoo, lots of towels, and a camera. (For safety, always supervise water play and drain the tub when done.)

513 crack a joke

Laugh out loud and you will find that your toddler laughs with you. Toddlers have a great sense of the absurd. Do something crazy, like offer a cookie to his elbow.

514 try a freeze

Teach your child about the transforming power of cold by helping her pour fruit juice from a lightweight pitcher into small paper cups. Then freeze the juice, adding wooden craft sticks once it's slushy. Waiting for these to freeze is difficult, but worth it. It's also fun to let the cups harden outside on a very cold winter's day.

515 solve a mystery

Hone your child's observation and logic skills by putting three plush animals in front of him and asking him to study them. Then have him close his eyes while you remove one. Ask, "OK—take a look now—who's missing?" Once he masters the game, make it more challenging by adding more animals.

516 get bouncy

At around two years of age your child may start being able to bounce a ball and catch it with two hands, or to catch one that you gently bounce to her. Just bouncing the ball is feat enough for a toddler, so don't be too worried about where it goes. And remember, larger, softer balls are usually easier for little hands to handle.

517 run a toy hospital

Two-year-olds are very caring and often want to fix things that are broken. Encourage your child's nurturing side by asking him to help you take care of plush animals or dolls. Let him tuck them into shoe-box beds while they recover, then get them all up to celebrate their restored health with a snack.

518 paint some rocks

Show your child how to paint smooth rocks with nontoxic paint. She can decorate them with abstract designs or turn them into creatures such as ladybugs, cats, or birds.

519 take a break

Sometimes your toddler needs you to help him understand when he needs a break. If he's worked up, take him away from the scene. Let him suck his thumb or clutch his blanket—or just hold him. Your touch is magic.

520 have a closer look

Give your toddler a plastic magnifier so she can see things she's never seen before. Looking at her own hand, a teddy bear's fur, or blades of grass will open up whole new tiny worlds to her. A small unbreakable magnifier of her own might even become one of your child's prized possessions.

24+ months

521 feed the birds

24+ months

Open a restaurant for the birds. Put up two or three bird feeders in your yard, making sure at least one of them is near your child's bedroom window. Let her help you keep the feeders filled with birdseed. Get a children's book about birds from the library and teach her the names of your most frequent visitors.

522 fashion instant puppets

Looking for a way to amuse your child fast? Use a nontoxic pen to draw faces on the pads of his index fingers. He can amuse himself by having his finger people talk to each other—and you!

523 make your child a star

Build your toddler's sense of self by videotaping her as she sings a song or tells a story. Play it back so she can watch herself in action.

524 have a drum session

Set up a bunch of percussion "instruments" outside or in a playroom. Include anything you've got that can be safely tapped, banged, or pounded: oatmeal boxes, pots and pans, tin pails, blocks of wood, cookie tins, dishpans, and empty plastic milk bottles are good things to start with. Offer your little drummer boy some spoons (wood, metal, or plastic) or a wooden kitchen mallet, and belt out his favorite tunes while he provides the percussion. Or just sit back and enjoy his extended drum solo. He's not just having fun; he's also honing his sense of rhythm and eye-hand coordination.

tip *Show your child how to vary the pace of drumming and how to pound out a beat softly and then loudly.*

525 paint designer shoelaces

Lay child-sized shoelaces on a paper towel and ask your child to help you add polka dots to them with nontoxic fabric paint (a pencil eraser makes a stamp of the right size). Once dry, lace them into her shoes.

526 create sponge art

Cut new kitchen sponges into strips and circles, let your child dip them into a small puddle of nontoxic liquid paint on a paper plate, and then press, drag, or dab the sponges onto paper. A sponge rolled into a tube and secured every 2 inches (5 cm) or so with rubber bands leaves an unusual impression when rolled across the paper. Try it out!

527 draw out hide-and-seek

Don't be too quick to uncover the kid giggling behind the curtain or under the table. Instead, say aloud, "Wow, if only (your child's name) were here, he could tell me what a cow says." Keep the game going with different animals until he reveals himself—or is laughing so hard it's impossible to pretend you don't know where he's hiding.

528 invent some rhymes

Start by letting your child finish familiar rhyming phrases, then add new ones. Once the concept is understood, take turns adding to a list of words that rhyme, such as cat, mat, bat, hat, and rat.

529 play nicely

Sharing takes practice. Once your toddler realizes how much fun she can have when she shares her toys, there'll be no stopping her. When you're playing with her, pick up and offer her toys and ask her to offer some to you.

530 deliver the mail

Mail may seem like magic to a toddler. Buy a small toy mailbox—or make one out of a shoe box—and deliver notes or small toys to it from time to time. Encourage friends and relatives to send postcards to your child, then drop them in the box. Sort through your junk mail for colorful envelopes to help fill his mailbox.

531 plant a carrot top

Cut the tops from a few whole carrots (parsnip and radish tops work, too—but not precut baby carrots) about 1 inch (2.5 cm) from the top. While carefully supervising, help your toddler set them, cut side down, in a shallow dish. Pour in water until it's about halfway up the carrot tops. Continue to water them every day. Soon feathery green leaves will reward your little gardener.

532 sort things out

Lay out 10 similar items, such as large beads or buttons, and ask your child to sort them by color, shape, or size. Then have her sort by more subtle characteristics, like the number of buttonholes. Be sure no small objects end up in her mouth.

533 hop on a magic carpet

Cut the bottom out of a large paper grocery bag, then snip along one folded edge to make a large rectangle. Cut a fringe into the two ends, then help your child color designs on this "carpet" with nontoxic washable markers. Once he's aboard his carpet, fire up his powers of imagination by asking him what he sees below. "Are you flying over the house? Do you see the swing set? Is that Tessie barking in the backyard?"

534 get picky

Place a dozen or so light objects—marshmallows, feathers, cereal—into a dish in front of your child. Give her a pair of blunt tweezers and show her how to pick up the objects and move them to another dish. This is a great way to sharpen fine motor skills, but since small objects are involved, watch closely.

535 paint a cookie canvas

Put a small amount of water in three bowls and add food coloring to each bowl to create three bright hues (the ratio of water to food coloring should be about two to one). Have your child use new, small paintbrushes to paint with these colors on unbaked sugar cookies. Once they're baked and cooled, let him eat his masterpieces.

536 eat some ants

Cut celery sticks into short lengths and spread cream cheese or hummus into the hollow of each stick. Have your toddler scatter raisin "ants" along the top of each piece. Who knew bugs could be so tasty?

 tip *Some days your two-year-old won't eat much, but don't worry: she'll know how much to eat, and when.*

537 jump for joy

Games and challenges that involve jumping are great for two-year-olds. They promote gross motor development, fine-tune their balance, and increase agility. They're also a great outlet for all that toddler energy. So draw a series of stars, polka dots, or flowers with sidewalk chalk, and see whether your child can jump from one to the other with both feet together. Later on, he might want to try hopping on one foot, then the other, or even try out the classic childhood game of hopscotch.

538 have a scavenger hunt

Give your child a magazine with lots of photos, then name a category—say, purple things, babies, food, or animals—and ask her to point out examples of those items as you page through the magazine with her.

539 whip up a smoothie

Have your toddler help you make a fruit shake with a handful of fruit (bananas and berries are especially good here), a scoop of ice cream or frozen yogurt, and a splash of juice. Mix well in a blender, making sure there are no lumps that could cause choking. A smoothie makes a great breakfast!

540 show off some art

Chances are that your little artist is producing a multitude of artworks at this stage. Here are some ways to display them. String a rope high (out of his reach) across a wall and use colorful clips to attach artworks. To showcase pictures on the refrigerator, buy magnetic sheets at a crafts store and make cut out concentric rectangles to create frames in a range of sizes. You can also scan some of your favorite pieces into your computer and e-mail them to friends and family, display them as your monitor's "wallpaper," or turn them into a digital slide show.

541 be upwardly mobile

By now your child is probably getting pretty good at stair climbing, though going up is still easier than going down. She might still like to scoot downstairs on her bottom, one step at a time, or walk down wedding-march style, so that both feet are on the same step at the same time. To build her confidence, practice going up and down together, but when you're not practicing, keep the stairs in your home safely gated.

542 explain change

Changes in your appearance can still be a little startling for your two-year-old. A hat or a pair of sunglasses might be fine, but if you were to color your hair or cut it very differently she might need some reassurance that it's really you. Explain the changes, and she'll soon adapt.

543 concoct a puzzling sandwich

Cut your child's sandwich into two or three irregular pieces. Challenge him to put the puzzle pieces back together—then let him reward himself by eating the sandwich.

544 pack a picnic

Do your picnic up right—basket, checkered cloth, and plastic cups—and never mind that it's just in your backyard. Outdoors, the juice is juicier; the cheese, cheesier; the carrot sticks, crunchier. Lie back with your child and search for sharks, trains, and alligators in the clouds, and you're well on your way to a memorable afternoon.

545 go out in the rain

Go outside every day, unless the weather's truly nasty. In fact, rainy walks can be the best kind. Put on boots and slickers and linger over (and jump in) puddles, search for earthworms on the sidewalk, float leaves in little pools, and tip your heads back and catch raindrops on your tongues. Sometimes it's fun getting wet!

546 make a banana split

Here's a snack that you can make together. Ask your toddler to peel a banana, then give it to you to cut in half crosswise. Help your child roll the banana sections in melted chocolate (make sure it is cool enough for little hands!), insert a wooden popsicle stick into each one for a handle, set them on wax paper, and freeze them for a half hour.

547 block out the pattern

Take eight toy blocks, four in each of two different colors. Lay out a pattern—say, two red blocks side by side. Give your toddler the remaining blocks and ask her to copy your model. Keep the game going by making a few more patterns for her to match.

548 eat what you read

Prepare and eat a food inspired by one of your child's favorite books. You could serve up a Dr. Seuss special of green eggs and ham, or Maurice Sendak's chicken soup with rice. Or why not taste a little of Goldilocks's beloved porridge?

549 wash with care

From time to time, that favorite plush toy will need a wash—but minimize your toddler's distress by washing it when he's asleep, and sneak it back into his bed before he wakes up in the morning. When he's awake, talk about how Teddy took a bath.

550 dine in style

Even your little one will enjoy fancy dinners at home from time to time, and it allows her to become familiar with more formal settings. Put out a tablecloth, let her help with an arrangement of flowers, play soft jazz or classical music in the background, and a meal of macaroni and cheese becomes elegant.

24+ months

552 make some dough

Delight your child by making your own modeling clay.

3 cups flour
1 ½ cups salt
6 teaspoons cream of tartar
3 tablespoons vegetable oil
3 cups water
Few drops of food coloring in three colors

Combine all the ingredients except the food coloring in a large pot over medium heat. Stir constantly until the mixture pulls away from the sides of the pot and forms a ball. Remove from the heat and allow to cool. Once cool enough to handle, turn dough onto waxed paper and knead it for a minute or so. Then divide it into three portions and knead in the food colorings to make each a different color. The dough is now ready for your child to play with. Store each dough portion in separate bags in the refrigerator. Discard after a week or two.

551 visit a farmers' market

An outing to a market is as fun as it is educational. Invite your toddler to help you find the things you want: "Can you help me pick out five apples?" Buy something new to eat, and let her make some choices of her own. Toddlers are more likely to try things that they've had a hand in picking out.

553 set up a command center

Write simple directions on slips of paper (for instance, "turn around," "hop like a bunny," and "bring me your toy cat"). Let your child pull the directions out of a plastic jar one at a time, and read them out to him. See how many directions he can remember and follow at a time. Let him select some commands for you, too.

554 share musical memories

Let your toddler hear the music of your own childhood. Dig out CDs or download some of your childhood favorites online. You'll be astonished at how many of the songs you can still sing all the words to—and who knows, you may keep the musical tradition going for another generation.

555 watch and encourage

Let your child take her time to work out new things, such as solving a puzzle. At this age she's becoming more self-reliant—and loves to be encouraged when she succeeds. Step in only if she gets frustrated.

556 have fun with felt

Purchase a felt board or make one by covering one large, sturdy piece of cardboard with felt from a fabric store. Then buy some ready-made felt stick-ons, or cut out your own from pieces of the fabric: geometric shapes, animals, people, clouds, trees, airplanes, robots, dinosaurs, or whatever your child is interested in. This low-tech and old-fashioned way to design scenes and tell stories is perfect for amusing a two-year-old.

557 shape some sandwiches

Use a cookie cutter or a knife to cut your child's sandwiches into interesting shapes. Or make a bicolored lunch by using one slice of white bread and one slice of whole wheat or pumpernickel.

558 blow a harmonica

A harmonica is a great instrument for toddlers to try out because it makes noise whether they inhale or exhale. Blowing up and down the edge of the harmonica helps them learn about musical scales while making up lively tunes.

24+ months

559 get the blues

Once in a while, devote a day to a specific color. If it's blue, for instance, dress in blue clothes, eat blueberries, color with blue crayons, and play with blue toys. Look for blue things wherever you go and make a game of pointing them out to each other.

tip *Learning to classify and sort objects—by color or size, for instance—helps your child make sense of the world.*

560 savor world cuisine

Get your child used to eating all kinds of cuisines early on. Many little ones don't like strong tastes yet, so start with the milder dishes: Chinese sesame noodles and sweet-and-sour chicken, gently spiced Indian biryani (rice) and nan (flat bread), or Middle Eastern hummus and falafel. Expand your child's cultural horizons by talking to him about the country the food comes from.

561 run a car wash

Encourage your child's instinct to take care of her things by helping her gather her toy cars and trucks outside or in the bathtub for a cleanup. Give her a small pail of soapy water and a sponge so she can wash them, then help her rinse them. For safety, stay with her and empty the bucket when she's all done.

562 wear a little nature

Outfit your toddler with flowers and weeds: make a necklace from daisies or dandelions, or a crown of wild grasses and flowers. If you live near maple trees, look for the seed "wings," which, when split open and sticky, make a great rhino horn to adorn your child's nose.

563 promote the chef

Let your toddler graduate to some real cooking duty. Supervise as he stirs up granola, tosses a salad, or uses a cookie cutter to shape dough. Make his sous-chef status official by giving him a pint-sized apron of his very own.

564 mess it up!

Your toddler will love it when she hears you make a mistake. Saying "Oh, hey, great red shirt!" when she's wearing blue, or confusing song lyrics ("Sing a song of sixpence, a pocket full of sky ...") will crack her up and promote her cognitive and language development.

565 get ambitious with blocks

Your child's ability to build with blocks gets a lot more sophisticated during this period. He now has the fine motor skills to build taller towers and longer trains. Show him architectural tricks, such as how to add spaces to toy-block constructions by straddling a cube across two slightly separated ones underneath.

566 design a private cave

Drape a blanket over a card table so that it covers all four sides to the ground, then tuck up one side to make a doorway. Presto: a perfect cave for one (or one toddler, two plush toys, three trucks, and a cookie). Throw in a blanket and a flashlight, and you've got deluxe toddler accommodations.

567 make a friend with eight legs

Create an octopus out of an old clean sock. First help your child stuff the toe end with cotton balls, then knot a short piece of string tightly under the stuffed section so it holds its round shape. Cut 15 slits from the sock's cuff end to within 1 inch (2.5 cm) or so of the string. Finish by having your child add eyes with a nontoxic marker, then take his new friend swimming across the "seafloor."

568 hop the animal train

Make a train by poking a small hole in each end of several shoe boxes and tying them together with yarn or ribbon. Let your child be the conductor of the Animal Express and, with her whistle blowing, help her load up her toys or favorite plush animals for a ride.

569 play "concentration"

Print out matching pictures from the Internet, lay them out faceup (four pictures—two pairs—are enough to start with), then turn them facedown and see if your child can turn over two that match. Add more pairs to keep the game challenging. Or try "Color Concentration," with pairs of colored cards, such as paint samples.

570 have a night out

When your two-year-old is up past dark, go out in the yard together. Spread out a blanket on the ground (snuggle under another one if it's chilly), let your eyes adjust to the darkness, and talk about the moon and the stars. Sing "Twinkle, Twinkle, Little Star" or "Fly Me to the Moon." Listen to the crickets, frogs, and any night birds that live in your area. And don't forget to keep your eyes peeled for lightning bugs!

571 make more of the shore

Under your close supervision, let your toddler feel the surf around her ankles, gently reassuring her if she's nervous. On shore, search for treasures, then sort them: shells, driftwood, and smooth sea glass—even creatures like periwinkles might turn up. Help her to gently examine the live things and return them to their homes. If she finds trash, there's a lesson there, too—help her take it to the nearest garbage can.

572 promote construction

Chances are your child is content with ordinary stacking blocks, but this is a good age to introduce new building toys. Look for toddler versions of construction logs and connecting blocks sized for small hands and safe to mouth and bite. Also have on hand a few toy cars and little people. Don't expect the Taj Mahal to rise on the playroom floor just yet. For now, the appeal is building cities and worlds that stay together for a while—long enough to show off to an admiring parent.

573 inspire a budding author

Your child may be starting to show an interest in writing by pretending to write. Encourage him, but don't worry about teaching the mechanics of writing just yet. Give him crayons and paper, and then ask him to read you what he's "written."

574 set sail for animal island

The sofa is the boat, and the floor is called Animal Island. If you disembark, you become an animal and must talk and move like one. Have something to say? Get back in the boat so you can communicate like a human being again.

575 try a coat trick

Putting on a coat can be hard for kids, so try this method: help your child lay her jacket, unbuttoned and faceup, on the floor in front of her so that the collar opening is at her feet. Guide her as she bends over and inserts her arms into the sleeves, then help her flip the coat over her head so that it lands in the right spot when she finishes putting her arms through the sleeves.

576 give and receive

Your toddler is starting to understand the joy of giving, receiving, and sharing. He will feel especially grown-up if you encourage him to give a present to his best friend on his friend's birthday.

577 tap out some water music

Fill six sturdy glasses with different amounts of water (add drops of food coloring for fun), arranging them from least full to most full. Show your child how to gently tap them with a metal spoon to make music. Demonstrate how adding or subtracting water changes the glasses' tones.

578 shadow him

Shine a bright light on the wall of a darkened room, and make shadow-puppet animals with your hands, using them to act out stories. Then help your child create some easy-to-make animal shadows of his own. Two good ones to start with are a rabbit (just have him hold up his fingers to show how old he is) and a butterfly (ask him to spread the fingers of both hands, holding them so that his thumbs are touching).

579 match colors

Expand your toddler's knowledge of color by laying out paper in bright crayon shades. Ask her to match crayons to the papers as you both name the colors.

580 bake a snake cake

Bake a cake in a Bundt pan; when it's cool, cut it into three pieces. Ask your child to help you arrange them on a platter so the curves form a slithering snake. Frost with green frosting, and have your toddler add half-cherry eyes and some sugar-wafer spots.

581 play "i spy" with your ears

Say, "I hear, with my little ear, two noises that are pretty near!" Ask your child to tell you two things he hears: a dog barking and a plane passing overhead, for instance. Make the game more challenging by asking for specifics, such as "I hear something that you ride in—what is it?"

tip *Locating an object by listening teaches your toddler to find an answer through the process of elimination.*

582 make bubbles

Pour bubble mix into a wide, shallow dish and demonstrate how to blow bubbles with a bubble wand, or shape your own from a pipe cleaner or toilet tissue tube (these get soggy after a while, so have a few on hand). Dip a plastic berry basket in the soapy soup and wave it to make dozens of tiny bubbles.

583 capture your child's day

Take photos of your child throughout the day, doing what she likes to do: playing, eating, going for walks, exploring the yard, picking up a sibling at school, helping out at home, and so on. Print or paste these pictures onto sheets of paper you can make into a booklet, or slide them into an album. It's guaranteed to become one of your toddler's very favorite books.

584 ride on a train

Line up the chairs in the dining room and invite your toddler—and any other family members who want to come along—to jump aboard the Chair Express, the fastest train in the house. Let him hand out construction paper "tickets" and collect them as riders get off and on.

585 be a patron of the arts

For a two-year-old, drawing is more about the physical act than making a design that represents a flower or a person. Praise her for what she's doing and how much fun she's having doing it. Still, it's fine to interpret a little: "Wow, that looks like an apple to me—it's so beautiful!"

586 dine with a worm

At a restaurant, create a friendly "worm" dining companion. Slip two drinking straws from their wrappers. Lay the end of one wrapper over the end of the other so that they form an L shape, and fold the one on the bottom over the one on top. Repeat, continuing to alternate folds until both wrappers are completely folded up. You'll have an accordion-like critter that can amuse your little one with its antics. No wrapped straws? Use paper strips from a napkin.

30+ thirty months & up

milestones

Your toddler is curious about his world, so be prepared to answer lots of questions!

- Running, jumping, tricycling, and playing catch help refine your toddler's physical skills.

- An increasing attention span reflects a growing ability to concentrate.

- Encouraging fantasy play and role play nurtures creativity, communication, and imagination in your toddler.

As your little one nears the end of his toddler months, he's becoming very much his own person. The speed at which he pick up new skills can leave you breathless at times, and there's no easing of the pace as he nears his third birthday. This is a golden age, with much of the willfulness of earlier toddler times making way for more relaxed interactions. You're still his favorite guide to his expanding world, so take the time to enjoy this special stage together.

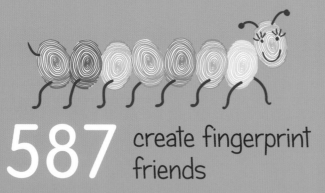

587 create fingerprint friends

Put out a pad of nontoxic washable ink (or nontoxic liquid paint on a paper plate) and ask your child to make fingerprints or thumbprints on paper. Once they're dry, use a marker to add details such as legs, tails, and petals to create people, animals, or flowers.

588 make sense of nonsense

When your child is feeling off his game, challenge him to look you straight in the eye and very slowly say "cabbage, cabbage, cabbage" without laughing or cracking a smile. Almost impossible!

589 mix some colors

Put nontoxic liquid paint in the three primary colors (red, blue, yellow) on a painter's palette or around the edges of a plate. Demonstrate how combining two colors creates a new one.

590 shake a stick

Scrunch a 5-foot (1.5 m) long piece of aluminum foil into the shape of a snake, then coil it into a spiral that fits inside an empty cardboard gift-wrap tube. Securely seal one end with heavy paper and packing tape. Pour 2/3 cup dried lentils into the open end, then securely seal that end, too. Stand the stick upright and listen to the "rain."

591 play mad scientist

Spread newspapers on a table and give your little chemist bowls of water, spoons, empty plastic cups, and cups containing a little salt, sugar, flour, lemon juice, or water. Let her mix, concoct, and taste, expanding her sensory knowledge.

592 build a fairy home

Go looking for fairy houses with your little one—are they under a twisted tree root, beneath the edge of the back step, inside a tangle of summer flowers? Bring the fairies a flat piece of bark for a table, moss for their beds, and acorn caps of water to drink. To help them upgrade their lodgings, use twigs, leaves, and other natural materials to build them a new home.

593 get heavy

"Heavy" work is great for developing your child's gross motor skills, and the accomplishment builds his self-esteem. So offer him a small pile of clothes to take to the closet or a sturdy bag to carry his books from one room to another.

594 teach scissor savvy

Toward the end of their third year, some children may be able to cut paper with scissors. To encourage the development of that fine motor skill, make sure that the scissors are child-safe but not so dull that they result in a frustrating experience. Teach your child from the beginning that scissors are to be used only with an adult around and only while seated. Help your little artist by giving her crisp paper (like construction paper) and holding the sides taut while she cuts fringe on an edge. As her skill develops, cut out strips for her to cut into squares, and then help her glue them onto colored paper to make a design.

595 cook up crazy crayons

Got lots of broken crayon bits? Line a muffin pan with paper liners. Peel the labels off the crayons and sort them, say, with all the blue shades in one cup and all the metallics in another. Fill the muffin cups one-third full, then bake at 225°F (110°C), watching closely, until the bits have melted. Let cool, peel off the liners, and then invite your child to use these crazy crayons.

30+
months

596 respect blankie

When your little one wants to comfort himself, his favorite blanket (or soft toy) reminds him of things that are snuggly just like you, and helps him to hang in there.

597 try out a different "i spy"

Play "I Spy" with a twist by focusing on what things do. For instance, you might say, "I spy something that plays music" (or that you can ride in, eat with, or sit on). It's a fun way to teach your child how things work.

 tip *When you're waiting somewhere without any toys close at hand, play "I Spy" with the objects around you.*

598 set the table

Help your child make paper cutouts of a plate, knife, spoon, fork, and glass (you may need to do most of the cutting). Together, glue them into their proper places on a construction-paper place mat. Take the paper place setting to the copy shop and have it laminated so your little helper can use it as a guide every time he sets the table.

599 pick a pumpkin

Find a local pumpkin patch that allows visitors to choose from a large selection. Wander among the gourds while talking about the different shapes, sizes, and colors you see, then help your child choose the perfect pumpkin for her—or several, in a variety of sizes—to take home and decorate. Don't forget to take pictures!

600 compare and contrast

Look at your feet and your child's feet side by side. Compare them in size, shape, and color, pointing out the ways in which your feet are different and yet similar. Showing him that he's the same as you in many ways—as well as unique—helps him develop pride in his body.

601 layer a parfait

Encourage your toddler to make a healthy fruit sundae in a tall plastic parfait glass. Help her layer yogurt, sliced strawberries or other berries, and something crunchy, like crumbled graham crackers. She'll enjoy making it almost as much as eating it.

602 get boxed in

Call an appliance store and ask if a large cardboard box can be saved for you—one that originally contained an oven or a refrigerator. With a box knife (in your hands) and crayons (in your child's), the box can become a grocery store, a puppet theater, a puppy kennel, or a castle. With the right props, his imagination can conjure up limitless possibilities.

603 put on a new face

Help your toddler place a medium-sized paper bag over her head, and gently use a crayon to mark where her eyes and mouth are. Take the bag off and cut openings at the marked spots. Set her up with crayons, nontoxic liquid paint, paper cutouts, and nontoxic glue so she can transform her new face into her wildest fancy, be it a tiger, a robot, or an alien.

604 go shopping together

To hone his matching skills, hand your child coupons and ask him to watch out for the items shown while he's sitting in the grocery cart. Offer hints like "I think you'll find that one in this aisle."

605 think variety

Encourage your toddler to try out a wide range of fun activities, from soccer or swimming to puppet shows and blowing bubbles. It will be years before her interests firm up, so it's great for her to try out lots of new things with you now.

606 be penny-wise

Demonstrate some fun chemistry by dropping dirty pennies into a glass jar with a lid. Cover them with vinegar, then throw in a tablespoon of salt. Seal the jar and shake gently. Help your child shake the jar again once or twice later on, and those pennies will be clean by the next day. Remind him that no matter how shiny, pennies should never go in mouths.

30+
months

607 blow a wish

Teach your child how to make a wish and blow the seeds off a full dandelion head. Use a magnifying glass to study the structure of the individual seeds. Then pretend he's a dandelion: make a wish out loud, blow on his hair, and encourage your little seedling to spin across the yard.

30+ months

608 cut out edible letters

Buy an inexpensive set of letter-shaped cookie cutters, and use them to cut out letters, such as your child's name or a favorite word, from a piece of cinnamon toast or a grilled cheese sandwich. Yummy (and secretly educational)!

609 create a paper-bag doll

Loosely stuff a paper lunch bag with newspaper. Seal this round "head" with tape, and attach a torso, arms, and legs cut out of construction paper. Ask your child to draw a face, ears, and hair on her floppy new friend.

610 assemble a car kit

Purchase an inexpensive metal baking pan, the kind with a plastic lid that slides on and off. Use the pan to store felt cutouts of various geometric shapes, people, animals, trees, clouds, and so on—all of which are great for imaginative play. Add a drawing pad, crayons, and large magnetic letters (which can be used on the bottom of the pan). Adapt the kit to your child's interests by including his favorite diversions, be they dinosaurs, puppets, or books. When you're hitting the road, throw in a few healthy snacks such as granola bars or boxes of raisins.

 tip *Loosely wrap some of his toys in brightly colored paper and have him unwrap them during a long car ride.*

611 trace some leaves

Have your toddler collect a handful of leaves from your yard or the park. Then set out a few crayons without their wrappers and some medium-weight paper (plain copy paper works well). Lay the leaves facedown (veiny side up) on the table and put the paper on top of them. Help your child stroke evenly over the leaf with the broad side of a crayon, revealing the leaf's image on the paper. Have her try using the same technique with other textured and relatively flat items like tree bark, a fossil in a rock, or the whorl of seeds in the center of a sunflower. Make a mobile by cutting out several of her favorite rubbings, punching a hole in the top of each and using thread to tie them along a chopstick or a dowel.

612 admire the ducks

Pay a visit to a duck pond to introduce your toddler to some feathered friends. See how many different kinds of ducks you can spot. If you sit quietly, they'll probably get comfortable with you and your child. With luck, they'll come close so you can get a good look—and a good listen to their quacks. Invite him to imitate the ducks by doing a bit of quacking himself.

613 sprout some initials

Help your child dampen a pad of cotton batting with water and lay it in a dish. Sprinkle wheat seeds in the shape of her initials onto the cotton and help her keep them moist until they sprout and her initials come to life!

614 explore snackitecture

Serve up a plate of snacks that double as building supplies: cheese cut into cubes, peeled apple pieces, cut-up grapes, marshmallows, and pretzel sticks. See what sorts of structures your child makes out of these building materials before he gobbles them up.

615 play crayon bingo

On your next road trip, give your child a small box of crayons and use them to improve her color sense. Ask her to watch the cars you pass, and when she spots a red one, to hand you the red crayon, and so on. When the box is empty, she's won!

616 enjoy a concert

Toddlers love outdoor concerts, especially ones geared to kids. Bring a blanket or some folding chairs, a picnic lunch, and a pillow and a plush toy in case the concert is a snooze. If it's lively, though, let her run around and dance as the spirit moves her, as long as she doesn't stray too far from home base—and your sight.

617 start your own bowling league

Improvise your own home bowling alley, using six tall lightweight cups for pins. Have your child help you set up the cups into three rows: three cups, two cups, and one cup to form an inverted triangle (great for counting practice). Complete your equipment with a selection of large, soft balls. Show your novice bowler how to stand back, take aim, and roll a ball hard enough to knock down the "pins." Strike!

618 clean for fun

When child's play turns into a major mess, enlist your toddler in a cleanup—but make it fun. Ask her to clean up all the square things. Or play "take 10": set out a timer and see how much she can tidy in 10 minutes (or during the length of one song), or ask her to put away 10 items—and then maybe 10 more.

619 use your noggin

Kids love figuring out which item in a series doesn't fit with the rest. At this stage, you can help hone your child's logical thinking by making things harder. For instance, show him a sneaker, a flip-flop, a sock, and a boot. The odd item might be the sock, because it's not a shoe. Or maybe it's the flip-flop, since you only wear it in the summer. The reasoning behind the answer is as interesting as the answer itself.

620 teach about opposites

Ask your toddler to name the opposite of the word you say. Start with easy ones: girl, boy; on, off; big, small; wet, dry; day, night.

 tip

Make up short sentences that include "opposites": the black cat is sleeping; the white cat is awake.

621 collaborate on a book

Your toddler is full of stories, so team up on a book: she dictates; you write; she illustrates. Put a few lines of text on each page, leaving plenty of room for artwork. Once you finish the book, bind her masterpiece in construction paper, then ask her to add some cover art and choose a title.

622 make an impression

Potato prints are always a hit. Cut a potato in half, and cut out a shape. Encourage your child to use nontoxic liquid paint to make his mark.

623 head down to the farm

Working farms that are open to visitors are worth searching out. Or perhaps you've noticed a place near you where animals graze in the fields. And a petting zoo with lambs and goats can seem quite exotic to city toddlers. Once you've found a suitable place, give your child a chance to see live versions of the animals in her storybooks. Wear boots, and always ask permission before attempting to pet or feed an animal. Wash your hands well afterward.

624 bake watermelon slices

Make crunchy slices of "watermelon" by using red food coloring to tint chocolate-chip cookie dough. Have your child help you shape dough into a roll and dip its edge in diluted green food coloring. Slice into semicircles. Bake and munch away.

625 try some tongue twisters

See if your child can get his mouth around these: *Toy boat, toy boat, toy boat, toy boat.* Or: *She sells seashells by the seashore.* Or this one: *Three gray geese in the green grass grazing.*

626 get creative with chalk

Carry some colorful sidewalk chalk in your car. Most park and school groundskeepers are tolerant about the use of chalk since the next rain will wash the marks away, anyway. Draw lily pads, so your little frog can hop from one to another. Make square "pages," and tell a story in words or pictures. Don't worry if the pavement's damp; colored chalks are at their most brilliant when wet.

627 jump a rhyme

By this age, your child might be too old for knee-bouncing rhymes—or she might not!
Five little monkeys jumping on the bed.
One rolled off and bumped his head.
Mama called the doctor and the doctor said,
"No more monkeys jumping on the bed!"
for subsequent verses, count down until you reach "one little monkey"
One little monkey jumping on the bed.
She rolled off and bumped her head.
Mama called the doctor and the doctor said,
"No more monkeys jumping on the bed!"

628 choose the right trike

First tricycle? Make sure your easy rider's feet reach the pedals comfortably. For safety, choose a steel frame and make sure he wears a properly fitting helmet. Spur your child's imagination by adding props to the trike—today it's a spaceship, tomorrow a fire engine.

629 grow a vine

Buy a sweet potato or a yam. Holding the yam upright, stick in four toothpicks around the center so that it will rest in the mouth of a jar with about half sticking out the top. Add water to the jar until it's about halfway up the yam, and set the jar in a sunny spot. Ask your child to help you top off the water level if it dips. It may take a week or two for the yam to sprout, but once it does, it will grow rapidly. Soon you'll have a lush vine—and your child will have a better appreciation of nature's magic.

630 be an answer person

This age ushers in an explosion of endless questions. Answer them as patiently as possible since they're the way your child is expanding her vocabulary and learning about the world.

631 test the taste buds

Try this sensory-exploration game when you're in the kitchen. Have your little one close his eyes tightly and open his mouth. Pop something yummy in, then see if he can guess what it is. A piece of banana? A chocolate chip? Now ask him to hold his nose and try again—what differences does he notice?

632 plant a box garden

You can use an actual window box, or just lay a milk carton on its side and cut off the uppermost side. Add some potting soil and help your child plant a few quick-to-grow seeds (zinnia, marigold, grass, and beans are all good choices). When the soil begins to feel dry, water it together. This is a good opportunity to start using a calendar, too—note the date on which you planted the seeds and help your child check off the days until the first sprouts appear.

634 walk the plank

Lay a sturdy 2 x 6-inch (5 x 15 cm) board or narrow table leaf that's about 3 feet (90 cm) long on two thick phone books, one under each end, so the board is roughly level and about 4 inches (10 cm) off the ground. Guide your child as he practices walking across it—then have him try walking across backward!

633 teach about time

Old-fashioned analog clocks often fascinate toddlers. Note that the face of the clock is a circle, point out the big hand and the little hand, and then count out the numbers together—reminding her that the little hand should be at "7" before she gets out of bed in the morning.

30+ months

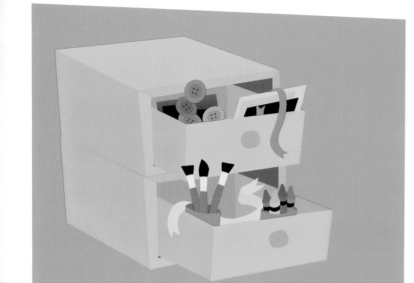

636 draw some finger actors

Create instant puppets by cutting the fingers off a white cotton glove and putting them on your child's fingers. Use nontoxic cloth markers to draw faces and other features on them to help bring the "characters" to life. Make a whole cast of fanciful folk, then let your toddler make up his own drama.

635 create art central

Stock a small chest of drawers or a bookcase with open bins containing child-friendly art materials, and your toddler will always have the tools to express her creative side. Include copy paper, newspaper, construction paper, scraps of gift wrap, and sheets of cardboard. Add plastic boxes of "found" objects such as ribbons, yarn, wooden spools, extra large buttons, and wooden sticks for making collages and other craft projects. Keep an "Ask First!" box of art supplies like nontoxic liquid paints, markers, and crayons—a repository for items she can use only with an adult's supervision or help—nearby but safely out of reach.

637 bathe scientifically

Scrunch a dry washcloth into the bottom of a large plastic cup. Help your child submerge the cup in the water, open end first, then raise it straight up again. Turn it over, and ask her to check the cloth. Discuss how it can be dry when it was under the water.

638 assemble a "bunny" salad

Show your child that making food can be fun. Ask him to put a clean lettuce leaf on a plate, then top it with a peeled pear half, cut side down. Give him two thin slices of baby carrots to stick into the pear's narrow end to make bunny ears. Add raisin eyes, a sliver of cherry for a nose, and a dollop of yogurt for a tail.

639 guess what's in the basket

Even an older toddler may not be ready for something as abstract as "20 Questions," but if you put a familiar object in a basket and cover it with a cloth, she might be able to guess what the item is with a few hints. Then let her put something in the basket and challenge you to guess the mystery item's identity.

640 dress with style

Kids love playing dress-up, and they don't need much encouragement to imagine themselves as bus drivers, animals, or magicians. Gather up old Halloween costumes, dress shirts, jackets, purses (ideally, complete with a wallet and business cards), and whatever other clothes and accessories you can donate to the cause. You'll be surprised at how much magic there is in your old winter hat!

641 get artsy

Collect the raw materials for a sculpture: wooden spools, clean wooden craft sticks, and empty milk cartons, for example. Then let your budding artist loose with nontoxic craft glue. Chances are your child will be more of an abstract expressionist than a realist, but at this age, most of the joy (and fine motor skill development) comes from just manipulating the shapes.

30+ months

642 explore from home base

Let your toddler try wandering a short distance away from you, then coming back on his own. Keep an eye on him though—he can move fast.

643 take in a movie

Sitting through a "real" movie in a big, dark theater might be a little demanding for a toddler. Instead, look for showings of short children's films at a local library or a community center. Or have family movie night at home with a DVD or a video.

 tip *Discuss a movie's topic with your child before and after the show—and, if you're watching at home, during it.*

644 play a xylophone

Buy a small xylophone, the kind with metal keys that are often used in grade schools. It will last forever, and your child will have a great time just puttering with it. And she'll sharpen her eye-hand coordination and develop her musical ear while she's at it!

645 decorate snazzy cupcakes

Bake some cupcakes, then ask your toddler to help you try out these fun decorating ideas. Add red food coloring to white frosting and use it to make the cupcakes look like apples, complete with a pretzel stem. Tint the frosting blue, frost the cupcake, then sprinkle half of it with crushed vanilla wafer crumbs: sea and sand, just like the beach! Turn a white-frosted cupcake into a baseball by painting on stitches with black frosting.

646 study the world of ants

Sprinkle sugar on the ground near an anthill, then give your child a plastic magnifier and invite him to spy on the ants as they gather their treasure. Do the ants seem to have different jobs? Are they a good team?

647 make instant friends

Introducing ... the foolproof origami puppy! Fold a square of paper in half, corner to corner, so it makes a triangle. With the folded edge of the paper facing away from you on the table, fold down the two outer corners so they look like floppy ears. Have her use a crayon or a pen to add eyes and a nose, and your child has made a new buddy. Make a whole litter of puppies, which she can decorate with spots or stripes.

648 team up to make dinner

Divide homemade or store-bought pizza dough into fist-size balls and, with your toddler's help, pat them thin and round. Set out bowls of tomato sauce, shredded cheese, olives, pepperoni slices—whatever your family enjoys on a pizza. Ask your little chef to take the family's orders for personal pizzas and let him arrange the desired toppings. You can take it from there.

649 map it

Teaching basic map skills stretches your child's cognitive skills and spatial awareness. Grab a drawing pad and take a walk with your toddler on your street. Take a bird's-eye view: "If we were flying, what would we see next to our house when we looked down from the sky? Right, we'd see your friend Susan's house. What else would we see?" Sketch the street and draw boxes labeled "My House," "Susan's House," and "Playground," for example. When you get home, cut simple versions of these landmarks out of construction paper and see whether your child can help you place them in the right order. "Remember what came next? The library or the hardware store?"

650 coach your toddler

Try these four steps to help your toddler master a new task, be it pouring milk or putting on socks:
1. Get her attention, then demonstrate and explain the task in simple language.
2. Give her materials that make the task easier—for example, a small pitcher into which you can pour the milk before she pours it into her glass.
3. Break the task into steps to make it easier: "Scrunch up the top of the sock first, like this."
4. Give her encouraging feedback: "You did that part just right—now pull the zipper up a little higher, and you've got it!"

651 whip up oobleck

Are you and your toddler ready for some messy science? Set yourself up—either outdoors or on a newspaper-covered kitchen table—with a wide plastic pan, two boxes of cornstarch, a pitcher of water tinted with food coloring, and a wooden spoon. Pour the cornstarch into the pan, and slowly stir in just enough water to make a mixture that's roughly the texture of cookie dough. You've just made Oobleck! Now let your child roll up his sleeves and play with it (you dive in there, too). Gather up a handful and squeeze it into a hard ball, then open your hand and watch it dribble back into ooze. *Note:* Don't pour Oobleck down the drain! When you're done playing with it, dispose of it by pouring it into an old milk carton and discarding it in the trash.

652 start a collection

Help your toddler explore her interests through collecting. A beach trip might spark a collection of shells; a trip to the park might lead to a pinecone collection. Or maybe she always brings back the same type of souvenir from family vacations: a T-shirt or a snow globe. Whatever she collects, help her display her keepsakes, perhaps in clear plastic jars or boxes on a shelf.

653 set up a pizza parlor

Kids love doing things that reflect the adult world they see around them, so encourage your child to try his hand as a pizza chef. Cut the "ingredients" for a pizza from felt: white cheese, tan dough, maroon pepperoni, brown mushrooms, and green peppers. Complete the effect with a few pizza boxes bought at your local real-life parlor. Throw in an apron so your little chef can serve his creation in style. *Buon appetito!*

654 look underwater

Make a viewing scope so your young marine biologist can study the shallow water at the beach or a pond. Cut both ends off a milk carton, cover one end with tautly stretched plastic wrap, and tape the edges to the sides of the carton with waterproof tape. Hold your child while she submerges the plastic-covered end into water and peeks through the other end. Hello, fish!

655 make a personal puzzle

Glue one of your child's drawings onto a piece of cardboard and cut it into a variety of shapes for him to fit together. Or purchase a blank puzzle at a crafts store and have him draw on it, take it apart, and reassemble it.

656 visit the playground

Many school playgrounds are open to the public on weekends and school holidays. Visit a few elementary schools, ones with playgrounds geared to the needs of smaller children. After trying out a few, give your child a choice: "Would you rather go to the playground with the pretend castle or the one with the giant turtle in the sandbox?"

657 create carton critters

To make a bug menagerie, cut a cardboard egg carton into pieces with different numbers of cup-shaped sections. Punch holes in strategic places, then invite your child to fashion bright pipe cleaners into legs, antennae, and wings. A one-cup section might become a ladybug; a three-cup piece makes a great caterpillar.

658 count your potatoes

To keep things fair in your toddler's group games, demonstrate the time-honored method of determining who goes first. Have all the children present extend their fisted "potatoes," and count around using the song "One Potato, Two Potato ..." to decide who is first.

659 number it

Numbers are everywhere. In a store or on the street, stop for a moment and say, "I spy something with a number 3." Give your toddler time to have a good look around, then praise him when he finds it.

660 belt out a funny tune

Relish the wordplay of this venerable kids' song:
I knew a man called Michael Finnegan;
He had whiskers on his chinnegan.
They fell out and then grew in again,
Poor old Michael Finnegan.
Begin again!

30+ months

662 ride through a car wash

After your child has watched the family car go through a car wash a few times, ask him whether he'd like to ride inside the car with you as it goes through its soapy shower. Explain that it will be a little noisy during the wash, and narrate everything that's happening.

661 shine some starlight

30+ months

Find an illustration of a simple constellation, such as Orion or the Big Dipper, in an astronomy book or online. Use a skewer or a small nail to poke holes in the bottom of a paper cup to match the constellation's shape. At bedtime, darken your child's room and help her shine a flashlight through the holes in the cup to project "stars" on the ceiling.

663 shake a bit of butter

This is a good family or group activity, since the shaking can take a long time and goes much faster if you take turns. Fill a plastic jar that has a tight-fitting lid with very cold heavy cream until it's two-thirds full. Drop in two or three clean glass marbles to help mix the cream, then start shaking the jar briskly. You can recite this old rhyme to help pass the time:

Come, butter, come,
Come, butter, come.
Baby's standing at the gate,
Waiting for a butter cake.
Come, butter, come!

Switch back and forth, taking over from your toddler when she gets tired or bored. In about 10 to 15 minutes, the cream will turn to butter. Strain out any remaining liquid, and use a wooden spoon to mix in salt to taste. Try your homemade butter on toast or crackers.

 tip *Taking turns and sharing are important social skills. A fun group activity is a great way to learn them.*

664 string some snacks

Let your toddler make an edible necklace by threading O-shaped cereal pieces, pretzels, and other stringable treats on twine or kitchen string.

665 park cars

Arrange pieces of colored construction paper "parking spaces" in a line and help your child "drive" toy cars onto them. Ask him to park each car on the colored square that matches it. Then mix up your instructions: "Please park the yellow truck in the red parking place."

666 read to the dog

Budding readers may not know all the words in a familiar picture book, but the dog doesn't know that. So sit her down with Fido and let her "read" to him. This activity works with cats or toy animals, too!

667 make some tiny friends

Watch butterflies in the garden together, and let caterpillars walk on your hands. Show caution, not fear, around potentially stinging insects like bees, and your child will learn not to panic at the sight of them.

668 tie-dye socks

Put a half-dozen pennies or marbles in one of your child's white cotton athletic socks, then do the same with its mate. Gather the fabric around each object to form a lump, and tie each lump off with a string or a rubber band. Mix fabric dye in a bucket (disposable paper buckets are available in the paint department of hardware stores), and let your child drop the socks in. Submerge them, following the directions on the dye packet. Rinse the socks well, then dry them in a warm dryer. Untie the strings and have your style-conscious toddler model his tie-dyed socks.

669 set up a puppet theater

Hem 3 feet (90 cm) or so of fabric by folding the top 2 inches (5 cm) down and stitching it in place. Thread a tensioned curtain rod through the hem, and position the rod horizontally in a doorway, about 3 feet (90 cm) or so from the floor. Voilà—instant puppet theater!

30+
months

3+ three years & up

milestones

By observing you, your preschooler learns vital social skills, gestures, and responses.

- Completing a task for you, such as sweeping up leaves, promotes self-esteem.

- Performing puppet shows and role-playing make great practice for talking about feelings.

- Dressing herself without any help from a grown-up is a step toward independence for your preschooler.

Growing independence and a wonderful way with words make your three-year-old a good-natured and fascinating companion. Eager to please, amuse, and help you, she loves making new friends, but she's still focused on her family. She is learning during every waking hour and drinking it all in: novelty and repetition, independence and closeness, the everyday and the unexpected. For a three-year-old, each and every day is a celebration.

670 be backward

Kids love silliness, especially when an adult joins in. So declare "Backward Day," and help your child put on his clothes backward. Walk backward together and you won't know whether you're both coming or going!

3+ years

671 introduce the computer

Draw a large square divided into three rows and three columns (like tic-tac-toe) on your computer. Teach your child to use the "fill" or "paint" tool to claim a space with her chosen color. Let her experiment with colors and patterns. To play again, paint each square white.

672 construct a riding route

If your toddler is riding a tricycle, help him to gain skill on his new wheels by using sidewalk chalk to chart a course for him to follow in an unoccupied paved area. Include turns, loops, and stop signs. He'll relish the challenge—and his newfound mobility.

673 glue a bean mosaic

Pour an assortment of dried beans onto a tray and put out cardboard, child-safe glue, and some nontoxic markers. Invite your little one to draw shapes and show her how to glue her beans on the paper to fill in her design.

674 pick purple

Have your child pick a color theme for the day. Say it's purple: he might wear a purple T-shirt and paint pictures of grapes. Then read Crockett Johnson's *Harold and the Purple Crayon* together.

675 look for animal homes

Read a book on wild animals' homes, then seek out some in your backyard. Promising places to look include tree branches for bird and squirrel nests, openings in the ground for chipmunk and mole tunnels, and the undersides of leaves for insect hideouts.

676 walk like a duck

Use yellow craft foam to fashion ducky feet for your child to waddle around in. Cut out two foot shapes slightly larger than your child's feet. On each piece of foam, cut two horizontal slits 5 inches (13 cm) wide and 2 inches (5 cm) apart. Slide her feet through the slits to keep the foam in place. Time for a duck walk!

677 jam together

Using a recipe for no-cook jam, let your child mash the berries and stir in the other ingredients. Enjoy the homemade goodness by putting out child-safe utensils so that he can make his own jam sandwich.

678 tie-dye paper

Accordion-fold a piece of paper into a long strip, then accordion-fold that piece into a small square. Dilute different colors of nontoxic paint with water to the consistency of milk, and pour each color into a cup in a muffin tray. Have your child dip the square's edges into different cups. Unfold the wet paper and allow to dry. See how the colors blend to make new shades?

679 brush up

Your three-year-old may now be able to brush her teeth with minimal supervision. Watch her efforts with great interest, and commend her on a job well done. You'll both notice how bright her smile is when she beams with pride!

680 make time for rhymes

Play simple games to help your preschooler understand—and relish—the magic of rhyme. Ask him, "What rhymes with *hat?*" "With *fun?*" When looking at a storybook together, you might ask, "Can you find a picture of an animal that rhymes with *big* on this page?"

681 get artistic

Help your child graduate from making flat artwork, such as paintings and drawings, to creating art with more than two dimensions. Give her materials like child-safe modeling clay to make simple sculptures of objects, people, and animals. Let her choose add-on materials for her masterpiece, such as an assortment of large child-safe buttons and pebbles.

 tip *Puzzles help your little one identify shapes of differing dimensions and their relationship to each other.*

683 listen to the night

On a night when your child is up past dark, dress him warmly or bundle him in a blanket and sit outside together. Hold him in your lap and ask him to close his eyes and listen. Does he hear crickets? Cars? An owl? Notice the different sounds and talk about the animals, vehicles, or people making them.

682 prep for a plane ride

Pack paper, crayons, stickers, a favorite soft toy, finger puppets, and books in a cabin-sized (and child-sized) bag. Add a covered container and a variety of snacks, including something chewy like a rolled fruit snack to ease "popping" ears for your little voyager. If you're traveling light, consider boarding later. That way she'll have more time to explore the airport and shake all of her wiggles out.

684 create a button bug

Read about insects together, or study some in your yard. Then invite your child to use buttons, nontoxic glue, and construction paper to make a bug of her own. Show her how to glue the buttons in a caterpillar shape, with a single larger button for the head. She can also add eyes and lots of tiny legs with a child-safe marker.

685 collage creatures

Cut body shapes of animals, such as sheep or ducks, from heavy paper. Put out some crafts materials—nontoxic paints, crayons, wrapping paper, magazines, macaroni—and invite your child to let his imagination run wild as he creates his very own menagerie.

tip *Choosing crafts materials and deciding what to create allows your preschooler to express his preferences.*

686 learn an animal alphabet

Sit down with your child and read aloud a book that uses animals to illustrate the alphabet. Then have her name animals that start with *A*, *B*, and so on.

687 talk with puppets

A puppet can help your little one express his innermost feelings. He may even put on a puppet show for you, too.

688 plant sunflowers

It's a flower and a snack! In spring, help your child plant sunflowers and see how fast they reach for the sky. Create a photo book: take pictures when she plants the seeds, when the plants push through the soil, and when the stems grow taller than she is. Then help her paste the photos in a journal. When the flowers mature in late summer, she can harvest and eat the seeds. Put some out for the birds and squirrels to munch, too.

689 watch feathered friends

Help your child use a simple bird guide to identify some of the regular feathered visitors to your yard. Soon they'll be as recognizable to him as old friends. Then give him his own disposable camera and let him take pictures to make his own personal bird book.

690 cultivate friendships

Invite your preschooler's friends over to play. To encourage cooperative play, balance free time with special activities, such as baking cookies, building a city out of blocks, or washing the dog.

691 make a car quilt

Have your preschooler help you cut (with child-safe scissors) squares from some worn-out clothes. Use pieces of fabric associated with good, warm times, like strips cut from old pajamas or flannel shirts. Stitch them together and then add a solid fabric backing to make a super snuggly car blanket.

692 freeze fruit

Here's a cool way to tempt your child with a healthy snack. Have him arrange favorite fruits in an ice cube tray and freeze them. Once the treats are frozen, enjoy them or store in plastic bags for later. Apple chunks, blueberries, pitted cherries—so many options!

693 get stuck on magnets

Gather several big magnets and a range of objects, from large paper clips to crayons. Ask your child to guess which items will stick to a magnet, then test her theories together. (Always use magnets with supervision and a reminder to keep them away from computers and watches.)

694 eat a rainbow

Go to the grocery store together and pick out lots of brightly colored (and nutrient-rich) fruits and veggies: scarlet beets, blue potatoes, emerald broccoli, purple grapes, and ruby strawberries. Once you've got the good stuff on hand, try together to eat as many different-colored foods as you can each day.

695 act out a bath-time story

Read to your child during his bath. If you pick a tale with a nautical theme, he might act it out with his bath toys. By the time you've finished a story, chances are he'll be clean, calm, and halfway to dreamland. (Never leave a child alone in the tub.)

696 watch a worm

Enough said. Just watch a worm with your little one. Earthworms are easy to find in the garden or on the sidewalk after a gentle rain. Watch them where they are, or pick one up carefully and set it into her hand (they're too fragile for a child to pick up). Talk about how the worm feels. Cold? Warm? Slimy? If you can't find worms, look for some ants instead.

697 fine-tune scissor skills

To help your child practice his scissor skills, encourage him to cut fringes along the edges of stiff paper. First, draw straight lines for him to cut along, then upgrade to more challenging wavy or dotted lines. Have him use kid-sized safety scissors, and show him how holding a side of the paper makes cutting easier.

tip *Cut out images from magazines or catalogs and invite your child to practice gluing them on a paper plate.*

698 be ambitious with sand

Three-year-olds are just coming into their sandbox glory days. The simple sensory joy of sand play is still with them (what feels better than running cool sand through your hands on a hot day?), but now their play is more purposeful: using tools and toys to pile, plow, dig, tunnel, and build. Sand toys don't have to be complicated. Spoons, cups, shovels, scoops, and water keep preschoolers busy in the sand for a long time. (Stay close by to supervise.)

699 dig for dino eggs

Use self-drying, nontoxic clay to mold egg shapes around small plastic dinosaurs, and have your explorer hunt for them in the yard. Then she can use paleontology tools (spoons and toy hammers) to uncover the "ancient" creatures inside.

700 read alfresco

On a warm day, let your child pick out a special book to read in a shady spot in the yard, and make it cozy with a comfortable blanket that you and he can sprawl out on. Don't forget cool drinks, since reading can be thirsty work.

701 string a bird snack

Show your child how to thread O-shaped cereal onto strings (knot the ends to hold the pieces in place). Help her hang them on trees and shrubs for birds to snack on. Watch as the birds flock to the tasty treats!

702 open a doll clinic

Build your child's confidence and sense of empathy by setting up a pretend doctor's office for his dolls and plush animals. Outfit it with bandages, a toy syringe (kids love giving "shots"), and a toy stethoscope for checking furry heartbeats. He may feel a little braver the next time he gets a boo-boo of his own.

703 house a bug

Make a bug-observation station for your young naturalist by cutting a window in the side of a round oatmeal container and taping a piece of netting or screening over it. Gently place a ladybug, beetle, or grasshopper inside for her to examine. Talk about nurturing and respecting tiny creatures before releasing the insect near the spot where you found it.

3+ years

704 nurture fresh herbs

Help your child plant herb seedlings in three broad clay pots about 4 inches (10 cm) deep. Thyme, dill, and oregano are child-friendly flavors, or he might like to try some mint. Set the pots on a moderately sunny windowsill and help your little gardener keep the soil moist. As the plants grow, he can pinch off leaves to enhance whatever's for dinner.

705 chart the weather

Cover a heavy piece of cardboard with blue and green felt to resemble the grass and the sky. Purchase or make felt cutouts in shapes that represent the sun, white and gray clouds, raindrops, snowflakes, and lightning. Have your child mirror the day's weather by adding those shapes to her grass-and-sky canvas.

706 make rock art

Take a field trip together and hunt for some interesting rocks—ones that are shiny, ridged, or unusually colored. Let your child wash and dry his rocks and set him up with art supplies (such as nontoxic paint and glue, yarn, and buttons) to make zany animals.

707 create a beach collage

Mark a recent outing—or conjure up the shore when summer or the sea is far away—with a do-it-yourself beach. Invite your child to decorate sturdy pieces of cardboard with hand-collected or store-bought shells and sand. She can paint the surf or make it from blue paper.

708 admire pussy willows

In late winter or early spring, take your child to a wooded area or a garden shop to look for fuzzy pussy-willow branches. Bring the branches home and put them in a vase for him to examine. They may even inspire him to make some art: give him paper and nontoxic brown paint to draw the stems. When the paint is dry, have him add puffs by dipping a fingertip or a cotton swab in gray paint and pressing it against a stem.

709 build skills

Build spatial relations, imagination, fine motor skills, and the Empire State Building, all at the same time. Offer your budding construction worker building toys: blocks, logs, interlocking plastic bricks, stacking cups, and empty shoe boxes. If at all possible, don't disturb her little masterpiece. As time goes by, she might knock it down—or create a whole town around it!

710 overcome obstacles

Challenge your budding gymnast by setting up an impromptu obstacle course where he can tumble over pillows, crawl under the table, and jump off a bottom step. Give him plenty of encouragement and support, and always stay close at hand to supervise.

711 say what's in a name

Play a name game with your child. First, tell her her full name, and then have her tell you yours (your first and last names, not just "Mommy" or "Daddy"). This information is important in an emergency, but for now keep it light by also asking her the names of her siblings, dog, goldfish, and teddy bear. Challenge her gently: "Are you sure my name's Beth? I thought it was Mom. OK, if it's Beth, is it Beth Cupcake? No? You're right, it's Beth Johnson!"

712 feed the birds

Make a winter treat for the birds by helping your child combine a cup each of soy or almond butter, cornmeal, raisins, chopped apples, and birdseed in a large bowl. Have him mix the ingredients and form the mixture into a ball, tie it up in a plastic mesh bag (the kind potatoes come in), and hang it outside for the birds.

713 dip a pretzel

Put out a small bowl of room-temperature almond butter or cream cheese and a plate of raisins, chopped dates, or coconut flakes (or a mix of all three). Teach your little gourmet how to dip one end of a fat pretzel rod into the bowl, and then dab it onto the plate of dried fruit to create a new taste sensation!

714 disguise math

3+
years

Slip a little math into daily activities. Ask your child to count out three eggs to help you make a cake or, while at the beach, to pour sand into a cup until it's half full. As she gets better at simple problems, casually introduce harder ones: "Andy and Amy are coming over, so we'll need a plum for each of you to snack on. How many plums do we need to buy at the store?"

715 bake granola

Have your child mix 4 cups (1 L) of raw oats in a bowl with a small amount of any of these: wheat germ, sunflower seeds, sesame seeds, raisins, chopped dried fruit, coconut flakes. Ask him to drizzle the mixture with honey and stir in a big spoonful of canola oil. Bake on a cookie sheet at 325°F (160°C), stirring occasionally (an adult job), for 20 minutes or until golden.

716 pack a lunch

Invite your child to decorate plain paper lunch bags using stamps, stickers, and markers. Or let her pick clip-art images from a computer graphics program and print them onto white paper bags (check your printer manual for the right settings). Then have her help you pack her lunch in a personalized bag.

717 capture the routine

Talk with your child about a typical day for him, then help him create a "day in the life" book with photos or drawings showing him in pursuits like eating breakfast or playing with friends. It will become a treasured keepsake he'll love to look at now and in the years to come (and it makes a great gift for relatives, too).

718 tug gently

Hand your child a piece of rope, a thin blanket, or scarves tied tightly together. Pull gently on your end while she tugs back, building her strength and confidence. Keep the game lighthearted by letting her tug you off balance and lead you around. (Stow away "rope" when you're done.)

719 have a q&a

Distract your child—while promoting his skills at logical thinking—by asking him specific questions about animals and nature. For instance, you might ask him, "What has four legs and says 'moo'?" or "What animal hops around and says 'ribbit'?"

720 improve trail mix

Have your pint-sized explorer make trail mix by enhancing granola. Add scoops of dried cherries or pineapple, chopped dates, banana chips, almonds, yogurt-covered raisins, sunflower seeds, shelled pistachios, or cereal. Then hit the trails!

721 pick your own

Visit a pick-your-own farm with your child. Blueberries and apples are especially easy to pick. Keep the visit short, allow a little snacking, and let her carry her part of the harvest to the weighing stand. At home, read a book about picking fruit together, like *Blueberries for Sal* by Robert McCloskey, and talk about your outing.

722 make yarn art

Outfit your child with leftover yarn of different colors, textures, and lengths. Then give her a glue stick, paper, and other kinds of artistic fodder such as buttons or dried pasta so she can create vibrant 3-D collages.

723 pose together

Head to a photo booth with your child and pose for some pictures together. Go for a different mood in each picture: silly, serious, or sad, for instance. Display the photo strip on the fridge or in your child's room. Or laminate it, punch a hole in the top, and loop a ribbon through the hole to make a bookmark for your child.

724 set up dominoes

Together position a set of dominoes in a curve, making sure each domino is about 1 inch (2.5 cm) from the next. Help your preschooler push the first domino over carefully and watch what happens next.

725 revisit animals

A petting zoo or farm open to the public may be more appealing to your brave three-year-old than it was when he was younger. Talk about what kinds of animals you see there and what they like to eat. Any time your child is around animals, especially unfamiliar ones, supervise closely, and always ask the staff or owner of the animals whether it's safe to touch them. Demonstrate for him how to move quietly and slowly to make the animals comfortable. Be sure you both wash your hands afterward.

3+ years

3+ years

726 befriend bats

Read about bats in *Stella Luna* by Janell Cannon, noting how they hunt using their own radar system and eat hundreds of insects a day. Then scan the sky at dusk for the nighttime flyers. Chat about other fascinating, useful, but not-so-cuddly animals, like bees and worms. Explain that each animal has an important job to do, like making honey or aerating the soil, and that most won't bother us if we don't bother them.

727 hop for joy

Jumping on one foot is a tricky skill to master, but your preschooler will soon be hopping everywhere.

728 pilot a plane

Introduce your preschooler to paper airplanes. First, invite her to use crayons or nontoxic markers to color her craft. Then show her how to fold it into an airplane shape and let it fly. Build her imagination and sense of geography by talking about the places she might want to visit in a real plane someday.

729 twist pipe dreams

Set your child up with pipe cleaners in different thicknesses, lengths, and colors. Watch his creativity soar as he twists them into sculptures. If he wants to branch out into mixed media, give him materials such as pom-poms, yarn, and buttons to embellish his fanciful creations.

730 get a blast from the past

Take your child's baby toys out of storage. She may have outgrown them, but she'll be delighted by a brief reunion with her rattles, squeak toys, simple books, and musical shakers.

731 discover color

Most preschoolers know their basic colors, but there's more than one shade of blue, right? Demonstrate sorting the crayons from a large box into different groups—all the blues, all the greens, and all the pinks, for instance—and talk about the color names with your budding artist. As you go through the day, encourage him to make up color names like rubber-duck yellow, marmalade orange, and beach-ball red.

732 care for pets

A three-year-old is big enough to be a good friend to cats, dogs, mice, and whoever else shares your home. Have your little one feed the family pets; fill their water bowls; brush and groom them; help wipe up their paw prints or spills; and even help train them, offering small food rewards when they follow instructions. There's no one like a preschooler to have the energy to run and play with a puppy.

733 count in two languages

Your preschooler can hone her math and language skills with this fun bilingual counting chant.
Uno, dos, y tres,
Cuatro, cinco, seis.
Siete, ocho, nueve,
Cuento hasta diez.
La la la la la. La la la la la.
One, two, and three,
Four, five, and six.
Seven, eight, and nine,
I count to ten.
La la la la la. La la la la la.

734 draw a reflection

At three years of age, your child is ready to try drawing from life—and what better model than himself? Have him stand in front of a full-length mirror, study his reflection, then draw what he saw. He can come back to the mirror anytime to refresh his memory or check a detail.

735 paint a song

Is your petit Picasso looking for inspiration? Try dancing and singing a favorite song together. Talk about how the song makes her feel and suggest she try her hand at illustrating those feelings.

736 stretch yourselves

Your three-year-old is rapidly refining his physical abilities, making him ready to expand his yoga repertoire. Look at a book or a DVD that has a wide range of poses, including old favorites like Downward-Facing Dog as well as new challenges.

737 freeze for fun

If it's literally freezing outside, fill a cake pan two-thirds full of water. Ask your child to gather evergreen sprigs or other greenery and lay them in the pan. Make a loop of twine and submerge half of it in the water. Leave the pan outside until the water freezes, then turn the ice out of the pan and hang it outside. If it's warm out, use your freezer, then later watch the artwork melt.

738 pack a bag for quiet time

Fill a small bag with quiet amusements that can pass the time in best-behavior situations, like a sibling's school concert. Small plush toys, finger puppets, rag dolls, and cloth books are good choices. Reinforce the "silent" theme by reserving the bag just for those occasions that require quiet.

739 press jewelry

Sit with your child and together form nontoxic, self-drying clay into a walnut-sized ball and flatten it. Have her press a leaf, a shell, or an acorn into the clay to make an impression, then peel the clay off. Use a drinking straw to poke a hole near the clay's edge. Let the clay dry before adding a string to make a necklace.

740 tell fish tales

Read some books on fish and marine life together, then take a trip to an aquarium or a pet shop. Look at as many marine animals as you can, talk about them with your child, and pick out your favorites. Does he favor colorful fish, odd-looking crabs, or funny frogs? Ask him which animal he'd like to be, and why.

741 play with words

Have fun with language by indulging in silly rhymes and alliteration. Ask your child to "put on your boat ... I mean your goat ... no, your coat." Declare her lunch "tasty tuna to tempt taste buds." She'll giggle at your goofiness and start thinking about (and playing with) words herself.

742 match clothes

Turn a household chore into a fun game—and at the same time help your child learn about matching sizes, colors, and patterns. When doing laundry, enlist your preschooler in some advanced sorting, pairing up the socks and separating the big T-shirts from the little ones.

 tip *Sorting, nesting, and stacking objects are all activities that develop your preschooler's logical reasoning skills.*

743 bring out a surprise

For quieter days when she's not feeling her best, keep a box tucked away that has some special treats to lift her spirits. These might include a set of temporary tattoos, some fresh modeling clay, a new water bottle (great for encouraging her to drink enough liquids), and a book of simple puzzles, pictures to color, or easy mazes.

744 puzzle out a frame

Recycle a puzzle with missing pieces by using the remaining pieces to get crafty. Help your child glue them onto a cardboard picture frame (store-bought or homemade). When the glue is dry, your artist can embellish the frame with nontoxic poster paint, glitter, buttons, or other trims and use it to frame a photo or drawing.

745 pot a pineapple

Teach your child about nature and encourage a green thumb. Twist or cut off the stalk of leaves from the top of a pineapple (adult job). Have him set the stalk in water for a few days until you see roots, and then plant the seedling in potting soil, watering it when the soil dries out. He'll soon have a sprouting pineapple tree!

746 bathe with letters

Give your child foam letters to float in the bathtub. Show her how to press the wet letters onto the side of the tub. Practice the ABC's and talk about the shapes, or just let her play with the letters to help her feel comfortable with the alphabet. (Never leave a child alone in the tub.)

3+ years

747 count out flapjacks

Whip up a stack of five silver-dollar pancakes one morning. When they've cooled, give your child blueberries and invite him to use them to "number" each flapjack, poking one berry into the top of the first one, two into the second one, and so on. Then ask him to make a tough decision—will he start eating the pancakes from one to five, or begin at five and work backward?

748 try new foods

Introduce new foods regularly so that your child experiences a wide variety of tastes and textures, encouraging an appetite for adventure.

749 swing away

At the park, choose a swing with a plastic or rubber seat and help your child get pumping. To teach her how to keep the swing in motion, gently guide her legs so that she's up in the air, then let go and have her bend them on the way back. Then sit on a swing beside her and demonstrate as you swing side by side.

3+ years

750 watch out for snowballs

Show your child how to roll balls of snow to make snow people—or snow dogs, cats, or snakes—and decorate them with carrots, twigs, and stones. He can probably trudge through the snow pretty steadily now, as long as it's not too deep, but do keep an eye on him. Be careful—you may find he can pack some pretty good snowballs now, too. No snow where you live? Make some with soap flakes and water.

751 paint postcards

Buy stiff watercolor paper at an art store and cut it into postcard-sized pieces. Show your young artist how to brush the paper lightly with water, then have her dab a brush dipped in nontoxic paint onto the paper. This wet-on-wet technique can produce effects that look just like sunsets, shadows, or reflections. When her masterpieces are dry, display them—or add addresses and stamps and mail them to friends and family.

752 have a sponge toss

Cool off on a hot day by tossing a large sponge soaked in cold water back and forth between you. Or have your child soak the sponge and toss it high in the air before catching it again.

753 bake pretzels

Help your child roll whole-grain bread dough into long snakes, then bend them into pretzel shapes. (Remember, not all pretzels look alike—make snails, geometric shapes, letters, or just twist them.) Place them on a baking sheet and brush with a little water, then sprinkle with salt. Bake at 375°F (190°C) for 12 minutes or until golden. Let them cool before munching.

754 chart growth

Have your child help you make a growth chart. Roll out a long piece of paper and paint a tree, a flower, or a vine. Then measure him against the paper and add a leaf, a bloom, or a butterfly to mark his height. Note the date and your child's age at the mark, too.

755 make it abstract

Have your little artist dip a piece of string into paint, and then drop the string onto a piece of paper on a washable floor. She can pick up the string and repeat the process—or use a new piece of string dipped in another color—until she decides her artwork is finished.

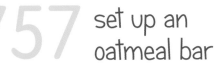

756 seek out sequels

Fuel your little bookworm's enthusiasm for reading by looking for sequels featuring some of his favorite characters, like the Cat in the Hat, Rainbow Fish, or Angelina Ballerina. The familiar characters will feel like old friends, and chances are he'll be eager to continue on to the next book in the series.

757 set up an oatmeal bar

If your child likes oatmeal or other hot cereals, it's easy to dish up a healthy breakfast. If things start feeling routine, surprise him with a breakfast buffet. Set out tiny bowls of mix-ins: raisins, dried cranberries, sliced almonds or walnut pieces, banana slices, and sunflower seeds are healthy and delicious options.

758 get a feel for letters

Cut the letters of your child's first name out of sandpaper. Invite him to trace the tactile shapes with his finger, building his familiarity with the alphabet and putting him on the road to spelling his name in the not-too-distant future.

759 assist animals

Three-year-olds are too young to volunteer, but your little one can help furry friends by gathering blankets or cat-food coupons for an animal shelter or by feeding a vacationing neighbor's dog with you. He'll love nurturing animals—and Bowser will relish the company!

760 catch a cookie

Adventurous three-year-olds admire the star of "The Gingerbread Man": the cookie who jumped out of the oven and ran from everyone who tried to catch him. Bake some gingerbread folks together, decorating them with raisins or chocolate chips. After the cookies cool, add frosting touches such as buttons. Then read the story together. Keep an eye on your gingerbread people so they don't run off while you're reading!

761 make sun tea

Make caffeine-free iced tea as a treat on a hot day, but let your child—and the sun—do all the work. Have her unwrap a couple of tea bags (herbal teas work, too) and drop them in a pitcher of water. Cover the pitcher with plastic wrap, then have her place it in a sunny spot outdoors. Let the tea brew for a few hours, checking on it until it's the strength you like. Serve in a tall glass with ice.

762 string a bead or two

Your child can handle small beads and fine string now, and will love novelties such as ribbon, alphabet beads for spelling his name, or photosensitive beads that go from white to colored in sunlight and fade indoors.

763 watch bubbles fly

Have your child blow bubbles as big as her toy allows—can she make a bubble within a bubble?—and then watch them take flight.

 tip *Make your own bubble solution with 1 cup of water, 1 teaspoon glycerin, and 2 tablespoons dish soap.*

764 dot ladybugs

Set your child up with some precut red circles (made of paper or cloth) and nontoxic washable markers, and help him transform the circles into ladybugs. He can add more buggy features, if he likes, such as pipe-cleaner antennae.

765 layer nachos

Nachos are kid-pleasers because children can put what they like on them. Have your child help you layer tortilla chips and shredded cheese on a plate. Then invite her to add her favorite nacho fixings: cooked shredded chicken or ground beef, black beans, or salsa. Microwave on low until the cheese melts, then let the nachos cool a bit before adding sour cream or guacamole, if desired. Now munch away!

766 eat like a bunny

Here's a surefire way to instill a love of healthy food in your child. Put out a plate of raw vegetables, and help your little one make a bunch of different dips using simple recipes. Explain that veggies are a bunny's favorite delicacy—and watch them disappear!

767 try an inkblot test

Have your child fold a sheet of paper in half, then unfold it and drop a few blobs of paint in different colors on one half of the inside. Then help him refold the paper, pressing with his hand. When he opens it up again, ask him what he sees in the picture.

768 design a fluffy friend

Draw the outline of a sheep with white chalk on a piece of black construction paper. Give your child a bag of cotton balls and nontoxic glue, and see how woolly the sheep can become. If she leaves the face uncovered, she can use the chalk to add eyes, a nose, and a mouth.

769 take a chalkboard to go

Cover the top of a hinged-lid box (such as a lunch box) with chalkboard paint from a crafts store. Help your child pack the box with colored chalks and an eraser, and he'll have a portable drawing center.

3+
years

3+
years

770 camp out

Have a family campout in the backyard, either in a tent or under the open sky in sleeping bags spread out on blankets. Roast hot dogs and marshmallows over the grill, tell stories by flashlight, and then snuggle down to sleep. If it gets cold or the night noises keep you awake, finish the night indoors. No yard? Just set up a campout in your living room!

771 grow beans

After the frosts, help your child poke four or five tall bamboo garden stakes into the ground in your yard, arranged in a circle about 3 feet (1 m) across. Use garden twine to gather and tie the tops of the stakes together, then plant a bean seed at the base of each stake. As the beanstalks grow, show her how to twine them around the stakes. Once they're tall and lush, usher your little one into her very own bean teepee and read "Jack and the Beanstalk" together.

772 piece a paper quilt

Talk with your child about how people make quilts from fabric scraps. Then have him use nontoxic glue to stick colored construction-paper squares on a larger piece of paper to create his own design. Display his artwork by hanging a string across a wall and fastening his paper quilt to it with clothespins.

773 get stamping

Sit your child down with some stamps (or just use leftover puzzle pieces or foam bath letters and shapes). Show her how to press them into a pad of nontoxic, washable ink or nontoxic paint and stamp letter designs or her initials on paper.

774 collage a shape

Reinforce your child's ability to recognize and name shapes by having him make a picture entirely out of variations of a single shape—say, squares or triangles. First, get him familiar with the shape. Have him help you cut its form out in different sizes from various colors of construction paper, wrapping paper, magazines, newspapers, or even fabric. Then help him use nontoxic glue to collage a person, an animal, or any abstract pattern. Can he use two brown triangles to make a friend's pigtails? How about kitty's ears?

775 climb like a spider

Help your three-year-old burn off some of her excess energy by inviting her to imitate different insects and animals. Spider stretches are a good way to start: ask her to lie on her back with her arms and legs in the air. Then have her work her limbs superfast, like a spider climbing a thread up to the center of its web.

776 swim for safety

If you haven't already introduced your little one to swimming, three is a great age to do so (and if you live near a pool or a naturally occurring body of water, it's an essential part of keeping him safe). You might start by taking a parent-child swim class. Remember that even after taking swim classes, no child should ever be left unattended near water.

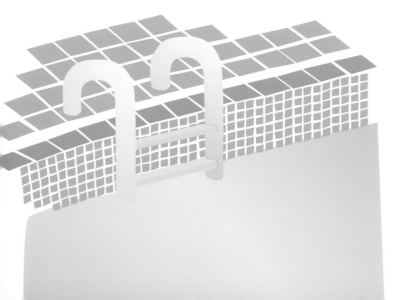

777 go on a scavenger hunt

Sit down with your child and come up with a scavenger hunt list (using both words and pictures) of things you might find in the woods or a park. The list might include a Y-shaped twig, an acorn, a white stone, a ladybug, and a bird's nest. Then take a hike to find them. On another day, you might make a list of things to hunt for in town. See if your little scavenger can find things like a planter full of flowers, a clock, a place to sit outside, and a fountain.

3+
years

778 make footprints

Place several large sheets of construction paper on a washable floor. Mix up nontoxic, washable paints in shallow trays and let your three-year-old dip her feet into the paint and dance a wild pattern right onto the paper.

779 do a blind fruit-tasting

When you're making a fruit salad, invite your child to join you and turn food prep into a game. Have him close his eyes and guess which fruit you just popped into his mouth. Talk about taste and texture. Was it tart like an apple? Or soft like a banana?

4+ four years & up

milestones

Supervised play dates are fun and help your preschooler learn to make friends.

- Expect constant chatter as he adds new words to his vocabulary on a daily basis.

- Pouring, measuring, and counting will all help him learn the basics of numbers.

- He is learning to identify the letters in his name and how printed words function in the world around him.

Because your four-year-old can better understand how things work, including the reasons why he can't always have his way, he doesn't get as frustrated. Proud of his rich vocabulary and equipped with a playful sense of humor, he can be feisty, but he also can focus on an activity and choose to stop and return to it later. Add in well-developed fine and gross motor skills, and he's is ready to take on the world, with you by his side to join in the fun.

780 save the planet

It's never too early to teach your child about responsible waste disposal. Have your little ecologist cut the plastic rings on soda cans so animals don't get caught in them.

781 complete a cookout

Make banana splits on the outdoor grill or in the oven. Slit the curved side of a banana (don't forget to leave the peel on) and let your child stuff the opening with mini marshmallows and chocolate chips. Wrap the banana in two layers of foil and heat it (adults only) for a few minutes on each side. Eat with a spoon when cool.

782 make a box car

A large cardboard box and some nontoxic markers are all your four-year-old needs to make a vehicle of his very own. Be sure to remove any staples, then help him add accessories such as paper-plate wheels and headlights made of plastic cups. Add a small pillow—and a small trailer for his favorite plush animal—and he's ready to go.

783 float a boat

Invite your youngster to use crayons to color a piece of paper however she desires, then help her fold the paper into a simple boat to float in the bathtub or wading pool. The wax from the crayons will help the craft stay afloat. (Always supervise water play.)

784 clap syllables

Teach your budding linguist about the building blocks of language by having him count the syllables in words with hand claps. Make it more fun by putting on some music he loves and having him clap out the syllables of familiar lyrics.

785 tote a tic-tac-toe

Buy a whiteboard or make a portable tic-tac-toe set by having your child draw a tic-tac-toe board on stiff cardboard, laminating it at a copy shop, punching a hole in a corner, and using string to tie on an erasable marker. After she plays a match with a friend in the car, at the park, or wherever she happens to be, clear the board with a tissue so it's ready for the next round.

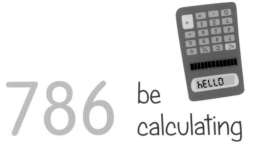

786 be calculating

Teach your child to use a calculator (one with large buttons makes things easier for little fingers). Playing with the calculator builds coordination. Plus, it sparks interest in numbers and basic adding and subtracting.

787 sculpt sand

Pick up sand in an array of colors at a crafts shop. Set your child up with the sand; clean, empty baby-food jars (with the labels removed); and a spoon so he can fill the jars with layers of sand in different colors to make multihued sculptures.

788 give flowers

May Day (May 1) is the traditional day for leaving surprise nosegays of flowers at people's doors, but it's a charming idea for any day. Help your child to gather and tie a tiny bouquet and attach a note with a friendly message. Then play lookout while she tiptoes up to leave it on a neighbor's doorstep before making a quiet getaway (well, except for the giggles).

789 visit a music shop

It's never too soon for the musical bug to bite your child. Take him to a music shop to browse, listen to customers testing out new instruments, and maybe try out a floor model keyboard, drum, or triangle. Don't want to leave without buying anything? Consider an instrument that's good for kids, like a kazoo, a tambourine, or a harmonica.

790 read true tales

Make sure your preschooler's library includes not just storybooks but also simple nonfiction books on a variety of topics. Preschoolers love paging through books about animals, transportation, or dinosaurs, as well as how-to books featuring games, crafts, or cooking.

791 construct a family tree

Have your budding genealogist draw a tree with several branches. Cut out circles from another piece of paper, have her draw family members on them, then help her use nontoxic glue to attach them to the tree.

 tip *Compile a family photograph album, including photos of cousins, aunts, uncles, grannies, and grandpas.*

4+ years

792 hit the trail

4+
years

A hike in the woods (or through local streets) is a full-scale family adventure. Set a comfortable pace for your child, bring bottles of water and light snacks, and take time to observe the plants and animals (or notable buildings and landmarks) you encounter along the way. Don't try to cover more ground than your child can handle—and make sure you all save some energy for the return trip!

793 watch history come alive

Visit a living history museum where actors re-create life from a different time or culture. Before you go, read about the period being depicted, and call to find out when there are hands-on activities for visitors, such as turning a butter churn or trying out foods that were popular during the period portrayed.

794 bead a bookmark

Help your child cut a foot-long (about a 30 cm) piece of hemp or linen cord (available at crafts or beading stores). Tie a double knot, one that's too big for a bead to slip over, about 3 inches (7.5 cm) from each end. Have your child string a few beads at each end, then tie new knots to hold the beads in place.

795 let the reading begin!

Your four-year-old may be ready for picture books with more text, and may even start picking out a few familiar words while you're reading to her. Encourage language pattern recognition by offering her stories that have similar themes or repeat key words.

tip *Read a favorite storybook as part of your bedtime routine. It's a snuggly, soothing end to a busy day.*

796 catch fish

Ask your child to draw and cut out a school of paper fish in assorted shapes, colors, and sizes. Securely tie a large magnet to a dowel-and-string "fishing rod," then help him attach paper clips to each fish. Designate a cardboard box or an area rug as a pond, and let your little angler bring in the catch of the day.

797 draw self-portraits

A great way to find out how your child sees herself is to ask her to make a few pictures: a portrait of her face, a drawing that shows her body, and a picture of herself doing something she loves. Label them with the date and store in a folder or album. Next year, ask her to make more pictures. If she compares them with the older drawings, she'll see how much she's grown.

798 clean up by color

Is there a big mess in your child's room? Turn cleanup into a sorting game by having him tidy up according to color. For instance, he might first put away all the red things, then the brown ones—then blue, then green, then white—until everything's in its place again.

799 create giant bubbles

Join your child in making giant bubbles on a sunny day. Cut a straw in half crosswise, thread a yard (about 1 m) of string through the pieces, and knot the ends. Head outside and dip the straw pieces and string into a bowl or pan of store-bought bubble solution. Holding the pieces of the straw apart, wave them gently to create huge bubbles. Now let your child try it. Once she gets the hang of it, she won't want to stop!

4+
years

800 put together a first-aid kit

So you're ready if mishaps occur, assemble a family first-aid kit together. Fill a watertight plastic box with antibiotic ointment, anti-itch cream, tweezers, cloth tape, gauze pads, and antiseptic wipes. Have your child pick a favorite plush toy to soothe your little patient—maybe a "boo-boo bear." He can even practice first aid on the toy.

801 bake "clay" dough

Shape store-bought or homemade bread dough as if it were clay. Make a snake with a pointed tongue or a lion with a mane. Bake at 375°F (190°C) until brown. When cool, it's ready to eat.

802 play badminton

Set up a badminton game. The "birdies" (aka shuttlecocks) are safe and lightweight, and she'll be thrilled every time one clears the net. If playing the game is still too challenging for your preschooler, just bouncing the shuttlecocks up and down on the rackets helps to develop coordination.

803 hurry spring along

On a day when the temperature's above freezing, cut some forsythia branches that are 2 to 3 feet (about 60 to 90 cm) long and drop them into a bucket of warm water for an hour. Transfer them to a vase of room-temperature water, and in a few days you'll be rewarded with golden blossoms—indoors!

804 start a scrapbook

Give your child a simple scrapbook (a binder with plastic sleeves will do nicely) for collecting whatever mementos mean the most to him, whether they are birthday greetings, vacation postcards, movie ticket stubs, blue ribbons from playing sports, pressed flowers, autumn leaves, or favorite photos.

805 outfit your young explorer

Have your child help you cut off the legs from a pair of her outgrown jeans or khakis. Help her sew the leg openings closed, tie a cord to the belt loops on the right and left sides to make a shoulder strap, and she's got an explorer's bag. Stock it with a compass, a magnifying glass, a pen, a notebook, a snack, a water bottle, and a kids' portable field guide. Then give her a good dose of sunscreen and a hat to keep the sun out of her eyes, and she'll be all set to explore the world's remote corners—or at least the backyard.

806 personalize pet bowls

Let your child use nontoxic paint pens from a crafts store to decorate his cat's or dog's plastic food and water dishes with some animal-friendly illustrations.

807 look for a four-leaf clover

Only one out of every 10,000 or so clovers has four leaves instead of the standard-issue three, but finding the time to search for one together on a beautiful day is already pretty lucky.

tip *By encouraging your preschooler's ability to visually discriminate, you're boosting her prereading skills, too.*

808 go fish

Deal out seven playing cards each. Ask "Do you have any threes (or sixes, eights, etc.)?"; your child surrenders all such cards or says "Go fish" if he doesn't have any. If you get a "Go fish," draw a card from the deck. If that yields a pair, lay it down and ask again. If not, the next player asks for a card. The first to pair up all his cards wins.

809 ride a pony

A four-year-old is mature and coordinated enough to ride a pony in well-supervised situations. At birthday parties and fairs, an adult should hold the animal's lead and walk beside the riding child, with the pony going no faster than a walk. At a riding school, safety precautions should include a helmet for every child and wood chips or mulch to pad the ground underneath. Teach your young equestrian to approach the pony slowly and calmly, and never to walk or stand behind a pony or horse. And pony treats like carrots should be offered only with the handler's supervision.

810 make a shell necklace

Stroll the shore with your little beachcomber and collect shells (or buy some at a crafts store). String the shells on a ribbon—presto! A necklace.

811 dig those rocks

Even if your child's too young to know her igneous from her sedimentary, rock collecting is a great hobby for preschoolers. Whether she specializes in mica chips, collects colored pebbles, or brings a special stone home from every vacation, she'll appreciate having a place to house her collection.

812 have fun in the car

When you're on a road trip, give your child a creative list (with small pictures, if needed) of items to look for: a cow, a bus, a barn, a lake, a stop sign, and so on. Have him cross off each item as he spots it. (If two children are playing, each child can count the items on his side of the car.) Tip: always have a new list ready to go.

813 grow catnip

Catnip seeds, a flowerpot 8 inches (20 cm) across, potting soil, and a sunny spot on a counter are all your child needs to grow cat treats. Once the seeds sprout (about two weeks after planting), snipping off bits to treat your cat will make the plant grow even bushier.

814 frame your pet

Create a frame for a picture of your family pet by cutting a small rectangle from the center of a larger rectangle of heavy cardboard. Help your child coat the frame with clear-drying, nontoxic crafts glue. While it's wet, have her attach dog biscuits, dry cat treats, or a layer of birdseed, matching the treat to the pet. Then have her give the pet food a coat of glue to preserve it (and so it no longer tempts your pet). When dry, glue in your pet's photo, attach a magnet to the back, and display your child's handiwork on the refrigerator.

4+ years

815 fill a book

Fold five sheets of letter-sized paper in half, tuck them inside a folded sheet of construction paper, and staple the "spine" edge to give your child a blank book to fill with drawings, letter-writing practice, tic-tac-toe games, or a story that you make up together and your child illustrates.

816 look at a leaf

Study a leaf together under a magnifying glass and talk about the leaf's delicate structure.

817 draw freehand

Teach your child how to make a looping, squiggly, freehand line using a black crayon on white paper without once raising the crayon, finishing so the line ends where it began. Encourage your young illustrator to use all the crayons in the box to fill in his drawing.

818 stage a show

If asked, most four-year-olds would agree with Shakespeare: the play's the thing. Encourage your aspiring dramatist to act out a favorite story with siblings or friends by offering old clothes for costumes and a clear space for a stage (since all the world's a stage, right?). Then sit back and enjoy the show.

819 be an archaeologist

Read or talk about archaeology, then outfit your child with some tools of the trade: small shovels or spoons, a strainer, a paintbrush, tweezers, and a magnifying glass. Hide doll dishes, dollhouse furniture, and other evidence of a fanciful civilization in a sandbox and then turn her loose to discover them.

820 count the days

Teach your child about time and scheduling by hanging a month-view calendar at his eye level. Let him mark special days—birthdays, trips, and play dates—with stickers or drawings. For each day, write what you're going to do or what you did.

821 host an almost-sleepover

Encourage your child to invite friends to visit in their pajamas one evening. After supper, settle everyone down to hear a story. Ask your guests' parents to pick them up afterward so they can sleep in their own beds.

822 work together

Preschoolers love helping out, so ask yours to assist you with chores. Get her a child-sized broom, for instance, and put her to work!

823 make a treasure box

Give your child a cigar box or shoe box, nontoxic markers, stickers, ribbons, and other materials to decorate a box for his treasures. He might even line the box with fabric in a related pattern, such as a baseball motif for a baseball card collection.

824 plant a tree together

Help your child plant a sapling, and visit the tree with her often to check on its growth. A deciduous (leaf-bearing) tree also lets her watch for seasonal changes. Taking her picture beside the tree once a year is a great way to chronicle her development, too. Someday she may even tell her own children, "I remember when I planted this tree."

825 play bocce ball

An inexpensive bocce game for kids is fun for your child to play, whether in the backyard or at the park. In fact, learning to roll or gently toss the balls close to the target ball is a skill that everyone in the family can develop together.

4+
years

826 design jewelry

A four-year-old's fine motor skills and emerging design sense enable her to make some pretty snazzy necklaces, bracelets, and rings. If she enjoys crafting jewelry, visit a bead shop and pick up a few special beads or look for a book on simple beading projects.

827 expand musical tastes

Your four-year-old is developing musical preferences at this stage, so it's a great time to expose him to different kinds of music. Invite him to listen and dance to classical, bluegrass, jazz, funk, and world music. Talk about the music afterward. What kind does he like listening to best? What's the most fun to dance to?

828 sculpt letters and numbers

Using colored clay, join your child in making different letters and numbers. It's a hands-on way to help her learn to recognize the ABC's and the 10 numerals, plus it's a great way to encourage creative sculpting.

829 get a library card

In most libraries, a kid just has to be able to sign his name in order to be a card-carrying book lover, so now's the time for him to apply for his very first library card. Once he's signed up, encourage him to check out the art displayed in the children's section, browse the shelves, and choose a special book. When you get home, he can mark the due date on a calendar.

830 mix up pink lemonade

Feeling in the pink? Invite your child to flavor (and color) a pitcher of lemonade with ¼ cup (60 ml) of grenadine syrup. Once she's stirred it up, serve it in ice-filled glasses. Have her top each tall glass with a pitted cherry.

831 take your crayons to go

Cut a rectangle of fabric from the seat of a discarded pair of blue jeans, making sure the piece you choose includes one of the back pockets. Then help your child use nontoxic glue to attach the fabric to the front cover of a spiral-bound sketchbook. When the glue is dry, he can fill the pocket with crayons and take his art journal on a drawing expedition.

834 make party poppers

Help your child cut a piece of colored tissue paper so it's wide enough to cover a cardboard tube widthwise and is 6 inches (15 cm) longer than the tube. Cover the tube with tissue paper, and then tie a piece of ribbon around one end to close and gather the paper. Have him put small, child-safe candies and toys in the tube's open end, tie up that end, and decorate his creation using nontoxic paints, glitter, and stickers.

4+
years

832 shoot hoops

Playing basketball helps your child practice all kinds of gross motor skills: running, dribbling a ball, passing a ball, and—perhaps the most fun of all—shooting baskets. To nurture your future all-star, put up a kid-sized basketball hoop, or find one at a park or playground.

833 grow seeds

Planting seedlings is easier than waiting for those poky seeds to sprout! Your preschooler will love the instant results she gets, which should motivate her to nurture those green shoots.

835 grill s'mores

Supervise your child as she toasts a marshmallow over the grill (a long barbecue fork will keep him a safe distance from the flames or coals). After it cools a little, help her sandwich it with a square of milk chocolate between two graham crackers. Rainy day? Assemble some s'mores and pop them in the microwave for a few seconds.

836 play marbles

Kids love marbles—counting them, sorting them, or just watching them roll around.

837 spot fish

Four-year-olds love learning about nature. At a pond or creek (and under your supervision), teach her to spot ripples on the water's surface as fish rise to eat insects. Putting on polarized sunglasses will give you both a better chance of glimpsing the fish through the water.

838 prompt with pictures

Photos—say, of your child brushing his teeth or feeding the dog—are a fun way to prompt him to do his chores. Help him choose and mount the pictures on posterboard to hang in his room.

839 keep an animal log

Read about local animal species together, then take a walk or watch from a window to spot some real-life specimens. Start a list of all the furry friends your little naturalist discovers, and ask her to draw a picture of each one next to its name.

840 create a creature

Join your preschooler in cutting out animal body parts and faces from magazines, then give him paper and glue so he can arrange the pieces to fashion funny and fanciful new hybrid animals.

841 string a telephone

Teach your child to make a cup-and-string telephone. Punch a hole in the bottoms of two paper cups and connect them with a long, thin string (such as dental floss) knotted inside the cup. Take turns talking and listening. If you use the cups with the string stretched taut, your "telephone" really does amplify sound.

842 step lightly

Teach your child how to make fairy footprints at the beach by making a fist and pressing the pinkie side into the sand. Then use your thumb and fingertips to add imprints for the toes. Make prints for right and left feet, or even make prints "walking" on the beach.

843 join the fan club

Fan-making is the perfect diversion on a hot day. Invite your child to decorate a piece of construction paper with nontoxic markers (she can go with abstract designs if she likes, or perhaps a frosty motif of penguins, polar bears, or snowflakes). Then show her how to fold the paper into pleats and chill out together.

844 befriend animals

Teach your inquisitive preschooler to approach animals safely and respectfully. Be his role model as he learns that the cat at the dry cleaner's can be grouchy, but the dog next door loves a scratch behind her ears. Make sure he lets animals come to him and gets the owners' permission before he pets them or gives them treats.

845 make a moose

Teach your child how to make a moose picture by tracing her foot (with her shoe on) and her hands (with her fingers spread to make "antlers") on brown paper. Then have her cut out the shapes and glue them onto white paper. She can give her moose personality by coloring in a big black nose and some goofy eyes.

846 splash around

Engage your child in some watery fun. If he's learning to swim, head down to the pool and play games that make the most of those skills, like retrieving floating pool toys or racing you from one side of the pool to the other. Or just stay home: the bathtub's a great "laboratory" for experiments aimed at discovering which kinds of objects float and which ones sink. (Remember to always supervise water play.)

4+
years

847 design signature specs

To increase the chances that your child will actually wear her sunglasses, encourage her to personalize them with small stickers, or use child-safe glue to attach charms or beads. Choose children's sunglasses that are labeled "100 percent UV Protection."

4+ years

848 go green together

Talk to your child about the environment and how we can help protect it. Then enlist him to make your home more "green." Together turn off lights, turn down the thermostat, put on sweaters, and don't run the water while brushing your teeth. Soon your young environmentalist will do these things on his own.

849 fascinate with fingerprints

Teach your child to be a fingerprint expert. Have her press a fingertip against clear glass, then sprinkle the spot she touched with baby powder, blow or brush off the excess, and pick up the resulting image by laying clear tape over it and pulling it up gently. Give her a magnifying glass so she can compare the whorls on the tape with her real finger. A perfect match!

850 encourage charity

Take your child shopping so he can pick out a toy to donate to a holiday charity drive. Now and again, ask him if he has any dolls, games, or plush animals he'd like to pass along to another child. Shelters, charity stores, and hospitals often welcome gently used toys.

851 transform seeds into art

Collect seeds in the spring or fall: maple wings, dandelion seeds, milkweed fluff, cottonwood puffs—whatever grows in your neck of the woods. Or just let your child pick out some seed packets at the store. Set her up with some sturdy paper, nontoxic paints, and child-safe glue, and watch her incorporate the seeds into a textured artwork. You might want to save some seeds to plant together, too.

852 pour milk

Encourage your child's growing sense of autonomy and accomplishment by letting him pour milk from a small pitcher (which is easier to handle than a carton) into his glass or his cereal bowl on his own.

 tip *Host a teddy bears' picnic and let your preschooler practice pouring using the cups from his tea set.*

853 get primitive

Share some storybooks about prehistoric times, then turn a grocery bag into an animal hide or a cave wall. Have your child scrunch the bag up, then flatten it out again until it's soft and wrinkled. Then outfit her with colored chalks for drawing stick figures of people and animals on the intriguingly primitive surface.

854 share tee time

Even a four-year-old can learn to swing a child's lightweight bat at a softball. To improve his odds of actually hitting it, use a tee designed to hold the ball at the right height. Be your little slugger's cheerleader and outfielder as he hones his skill.

855 stencil a shirt

Have your child cut a geometric or animal shape out of heavy paper. Use masking tape to attach it to the front of a light-colored T-shirt. While wearing old clothes, your child can dip a large paintbrush into fabric paint and rub her finger along the bristles to spray paint around the shape. When she's done, remove the stencil, let the shirt dry, then set the image by putting the shirt in a dryer on low heat.

856 festoon a room

Help your child fold squares of colorful tissue paper into fans, in quarters or eighths, and show him how to cut shapes out of the edges, much as you'd cut out paper snowflakes. Unfold the paper and together hang the designs on a line of string.

4+ years

857 practice kicking a ball

It may look simple, but kicking a ball is a feat of precision, eye-foot coordination, balance, and muscle control. Kick the ball gently toward your preschooler and have her kick it back your way. Her dexterity and ball skills will improve quickly with practice.

858 tie shoelaces

Encourage your little one to start tying his own shoelaces. The fine finger movements and control necessary are best practiced when you're not rushing out somewhere—let him take his time on this one!

4+
years

860 love the lovie

Even as your child ventures out into the world more independently, he might still appreciate the chance to reassure himself with a special blanket or cuddly toy he associates with home and family. Let him take his lovie with him whenever he wants, since it helps him feel safe while he's pushing his boundaries.

861 count with number towers

Help your child cut five "towers" from colored paper and have her write the numbers 1 through 10 from the bottom to the top of the first tower. On the next, start at the bottom and count together as she writes 11 through 20. Keep going, with each tower containing the next 10 numbers. Arrange the towers side by side to help your child count by tens. Hang them on her wall, and soon she'll have no trouble counting.

859 craft a show

Set aside a special day when your child invites a few friends over to make crafty items like picture frames, necklaces, paintings—or whatever captures each young artist's imagination. Then set up a table or two outside and display their handiwork. Who knows, they might even make some sales to your neighbors!

862 call home

Teach your child your home phone number, and let him practice calling it from your house (he'll get your voice mail or a busy signal) and from other phones, including cell phones. This is also a good time to remind him to call 911 in an emergency.

863 bake monkey bread

If you make bread dough for a basic white loaf and melt the butter, your child can do the rest, except when the oven is involved. Have your child break off pieces of dough, roll them into walnut-sized balls, and dip them into a bowl containing cooled melted butter. Next, have her drop the buttery balls of dough into a Bundt pan, layering them until the pan is two-thirds full. Bake as directed. Once the bread has cooled, remove it from the pan and invite her to dive in and pull the balls apart with her hands—the way a monkey would. For a yummy sweet variation, have your child roll each dough ball in cinnamon and sugar before placing it in the pan.

864 make multilingual wishes

Teach your child to say "happy birthday" to family and friends in a few different languages.
Arabic: *Eeid milad sa'aeed*
(AID mee-LAHD sah-ah-YEED)
French: *bon anniversaire*
(BUN ah-nee-vehr-SEHR)
Japanese: *otanjou-bi omedetou gozaimasu*
(oh-tahn-jo-bee oh-meh-deh-toh go-zah-ee-MAHS)
Spanish: *feliz cumpleaños*
(feh-LEECE coom-pleh-AH-nyohs)

865 have a heart

Show your preschooler how to make hearts by cutting a teardrop shape along the edge of a folded piece of paper. Get him started by drawing the cutting line for him; before you know it he'll be turning out dozens of hearts for cards and crafts projects all by himself.

866 show your dog who's boss

If you have a dog, it's important to make sure he minds your child the same way he does older family members. A fun training activity is for you and your child to go to different rooms, each with a few special dog treats. Take turns calling, "Jake! Come!" and reward your pet with treats when he responds. As a bonus, your dog gets a good workout while he learns.

867 enjoy a game of checkers

Four is a wonderful age to learn checkers—a great game for people of different generations to play together. Play at home or pack a portable set whenever you go out. Checkers is an amusing way to pass the time—say, while you're waiting for a meal in a restaurant.

868 bottle the ocean

Fill a clear plastic bottle halfway with blue-tinted water, add a toy boat or plastic fish, then fill almost to the top with mineral oil. Apply hot glue to the neck of the bottle with a glue gun (adults only), screw on the lid, and let the glue set. Lay the bottle on its side, then invite your child to rock it gently to make "waves."

869 be prepared

Playing "What if ..." is a good way to teach your child how to handle emergencies. Ask, "What if you see someone who looks badly hurt?" (Tell an adult or call 911.) "What if a ball rolls into the street?" (Ask an adult to get it.) "What if the kitty scratches you?" (Ask an adult for some first-aid help—and a hug to make it all better.)

870 add it up

Learning math doesn't have to involve paper, blackboards, or calculators. Lay the foundation for learning about fractions by pointing out the difference between a half and a whole cup, the way the pizza is divided into eight slices, or the fact that sharing four cookies with a friend means that they each get two.

871 host a backyard contest

Gather some of your child's friends together and set up a circuit of active games for them. You might want to include an obstacle course of hula hoops laid flat on the grass to hop through, a garden hose stretched out as a "beam" to walk across, beanbags and wet sponges to toss, or other kid-pleasing activities. Start a child or two off on each activity. When you blow a whistle, have each child move on to the next activity.

872 write with light

Have your child lie on her back in a darkened room (with you there for company, of course) and invite her to use a small flashlight to "write" letters or draw simple pictures on the ceiling. See if you can guess what she's writing. Take turns writing and guessing.

873 fill in the speech balloons

Look for pictures of people in old newspapers or magazines and help your child glue cartoon speech balloons into the scene. Talk about what the people are doing, then have your child dictate the dialogue.

 tip *Invite your child to invent dialogue and imagine what someone else might feel, to encourage empathy.*

4+ years

874 race with drinking straws

Draw an obstacle course in chalk on a sidewalk, then show your child how to race a small piece of crumpled paper or foil through the course by blowing on it through a drinking straw. He can compete with you or a friend to be the first to blow across the finish line.

875 exit gracefully

Help your preschooler make a smooth transition when it's time to end a fun event like a play date. Give her some warning ("We'll have to go home in 15 minutes") and a couple of notices ("Let's find your shoes now, because it's almost time to go"), and encourage her as she learns to leave quickly and without any fuss.

876 protect your veggie patch

Save scratched CDs or any that come in your junk mail, then help your child affix twine to hang them from branches or stakes in your vegetable garden. As your CDs spin and twinkle in the sunlight, they'll keep birds from eating the fruits of your labors.

877 catch and release

If you're lucky enough to live in an area that has fireflies during the summer, help your child catch some during a balmy evening. Besides giving off an enchanting glow, fireflies fly slowly and don't bite, so they're ideal subjects for informal nature study. House them temporarily in a glass jar (punch tiny holes in the lid to let in air). Let your child study the living lanterns for an hour or so, then let them go so they can get on with their buggy adventures.

4+
years

878 recite poetry

Read your child some great poetry: works by Shel Silverstein, Robert Louis Stevenson, Douglas Florian, Jack Prelutsky, and many others are friendly, funny, and easy for four-year-olds to understand and enjoy.

879 climb higher

Seek out school or park playgrounds with such climbing equipment as monkey bars, a tall net, a firefighter's pole, or even a low rock-climbing wall. Supervise your child as he goes up and down, over and under—and improves his gross motor skills along the way.

880 practice somersaults

Find a safe spot of soft ground and gently help your little one tuck his head under and roll over. Somersaults are great fun!

881 design a paperweight

Have your child cut out a photo she likes from a magazine or catalog and affix it to a smooth stone with nontoxic glue. To keep the picture from yellowing, thin some more glue with a little water and have her paint it over the picture with a small paintbrush. When the glue's dry, she'll have her own personal desk accessory.

882 hang out at the firehouse

Call ahead to arrange a visit for your child (and maybe some of his friends) to check out your local fire station. Depending on what's going on when you arrive, he may be able to see the fire trucks close up, watch them being washed and serviced, or talk with firefighters. Some stations offer small gifts like coloring books or plastic firefighter's helmets to kids who visit.

883 remember your lines

When you find yourself reading the same book again and again, pause occasionally and ask your child what she thinks will happen next. Or stop before the end of each sentence and allow her to finish the line. Repetition can be to her advantage: she can show off her memory!

884 exercise creative license

Challenge your child to make a silly phrase using the letters on the license plate of the car in front of yours. For instance, if the license plate has the letters "TLB" on it, he might come up with "turtles love ballet."

885 make a piggy bank

Cut a slit in the plastic top of a tall, cylindrical potato chip can. Help your child cover the sides of the can with wrapping paper. Hold the paper in place for her while she tapes it around the can (or switch roles, if that's easier for her). Now that she's got her homemade piggy bank, talk to her about how money works (toys don't grow on trees!) and encourage her to start saving some of her own. She might even earn a few coins by doing extra chores around the house or in the yard.

886 swap books

Invite a small group of parents and kids to join you and your child in a book swap. Ask each attendee to bring several good used books to trade (don't ask your child to part with special favorites—and you can hold on to yours, too). Leave some books and take some, and share a snack and maybe a story or two. Everyone goes home with new reading material—for free!

887 tuck in those corners

Believe it or not, your little one will love making his bed all by himself in the morning. See? No wrinkles! (Or not very many.)

888 make a special paper doll

Cut out your child's head and face from a snapshot (the bigger the better). Draw a simple body shape on stiff posterboard, then help her glue on the photo cutout to make a paper doll. Using lighter paper, trace around the body shape to make simple clothing shapes she can cut out and color as she wishes. Use a reusable-glue stick (similar to the not-too-sticky adhesive used in sticky notes) to make the clothes easy to put on and take off. Got a group shot of your child with her playmates or siblings? Your child can make some familiar friends for her doll.

889 be inspired by books

Read some books together by renowned kids' author Eric Carle (*The Very Hungry Caterpillar* and *The Very Busy Spider* are some of his popular titles) and try out his style of collage. Finger paint different patterns on white or colored paper, then cut and paste the patterns into collages of animal and nature shapes.

890 set up a work space

4+ years

Dedicate a space where your child can draw, write, and dream. Having a spot devoted to those pursuits reinforces their importance while giving him a sense of ownership, independence, and maturity. Encourage him to personalize his work space, for example, by decorating plastic cups with colored paper or tape to make holders for crayons or pencils.

5+
years

5+ five years & up

milestones

Whatever your child's favorite activities are, she learns best through play.

- Problem-solving skills help expand your five-year-old's repertoire of play.

- Your little one will have a ready appetite for new experiences and adventures.

- Expanding brainpower means that your five-year-old's memory and coordination are improving, too.

At age five, literacy takes a giant leap, coordination improves, and concentration increases—in fact, your child is more adept at just about everything. Her vocabulary of about 5,000 words lets her tell incredibly detailed stories. Her social circle expands to include new friends, and her view of the world is growing larger, too, as shown by her increased concern for animals. But even with her expanding horizons, in your child's book, you're still number one.

891 go nutty

Ask your child to assist you as you measure and pour 2 cups (475 ml) of salted, roasted almonds or cashews (not peanuts) into a blender or food processor. Blend until smooth. Let her use a butter knife to spread the nut butter on crackers or bread—enough for both of you!

892 play "slap jack"

Deal out a standard deck of 52 cards evenly between you and your child, but don't look at them yet. Taking turns, pick up a card from your stack and lay it faceup on the table to create a third stack. If the card is a jack, the goal is to try to place your hand on top of it before your opponent does, winning you the jack and all the cards under it. The winner is the player who ends up with all of the cards.

893 learn to jump rope

Have your child start with the rope on the ground behind him. Then have him swing it over his head to the ground in front of him, then jump over it as it lies there. Practice (and a few demos) will soon have him jumping on his own.

894 read all about it

Take dictation from your child to produce a few short news stories about your family's exploits using a simple computer publishing program (or just your best handwriting on a piece of paper). Add a masthead and headlines, then ask her to make some illustrations (or help you pick out a few photos) to accompany the articles for your family gazette.

895 create collages

Collage basics are cardboard for a foundation, scissors, plenty of nontoxic glue, and, of course, imagination. Beyond that, collages can be made of just about anything: wrapping paper, ribbons, buttons, stickers, pictures cut from magazines, and paint samples. Or use materials like bark, seeds, leaves, grasses, and pressed flowers. Or suggest a collage of pictures of foods he enjoys, a seasonal motif such as spring flowers or autumn leaves, or just a mix of assorted items in his favorite colors.

896 make shoe-venirs

If you've got an old pair of your child's sneakers and a permanent marker on hand, your child can use them to gather her friends' signatures, marking a special event.

897 assemble a book

Use a three-hole punch to make holes in about a dozen sheets of white drawing paper and put them in a binder. For a cover, ask your child to draw a picture on a sheet of paper and help him attach it to the front of the binder with child-safe glue. He can draw, doodle, and write in his new book. You can jump-start literacy by having him dictate words for you to write on the pages.

898 craft a felt necklace

Teach your child how to make a necklace by first cutting felt into small squares, triangles, or any other shape she fancies. Then help her use a child-safe crafts needle and sturdy thread to string the shapes together into a necklace.

899 leaf through a scrapbook

Take a stroll outside with your child and invite him to pick up leaves that appeal to him. He can press them into a scrapbook at home, and together you can use a guide to identify the trees they came from. To help him learn about seasonal change, go on another excursion to collect leaves during a different time of year.

900 design snowflakes

Teach your child to fold circles or squares of thin paper and cut slashes and shapes into both the open and the folded sides to make snowy designs. For a shimmering effect, have her dab the snowflakes with a glue stick and sprinkle them with silver glitter.

901 create a comb kazoo

Give your child a clean, fine-tooth pocket comb and a piece of thin, strong paper. (Wax paper works well, but you can also try experimenting with other types.) Have her wrap the comb's teeth in the paper, then press her lips gently against the paper and hum strongly to make a hair-raising tune.

902 write a safety guide

Have a family safety drill covering topics such as where to meet in case everyone has to leave the house quickly. Ask your child to take snapshots of key parts of the route with a disposable camera and paste the photos on paper. Then have him dictate the captions for his home-safety manual.

 tip *A five-year-old can begin to handle a grown-up's camera—with close supervision, of course.*

5+ years

903 make silhouettes

Tape a piece of white paper to a wall, darken the room, and ask your child to sit about 2 feet (60 cm) in front of the paper. Shine a bright light at the side of his face (have him close his eyes). Outline his shadow on the white paper, then have him cut out the outline, place it on a piece of black construction paper, and trace around it. Next he can cut out the black silhouette and glue it to a white piece of paper. Then let him seat you or a stuffed animal with a distinctive profile on the chair and trace and cut out its silhouette.

904 picture the alphabet

Look through old magazines together for photos that illustrate letters of the alphabet: an ape for *A*, a ball for *B*, and so on. For do-it-yourself flash cards, have your child paste pictures or photos on cardboard with nontoxic glue, and write the letter on the back.

905 draw a finger puppet

Show your child how to transform her hand into a finger puppet by planting the tips of her thumb, pointer, ring, and pinkie fingers on the table to make the legs of a "creature," using her middle finger to form its head and long neck. Draw a simple face on the tip of her middle finger with a washable nontoxic marker, and see if she can walk the creature across the table. Sound effects like growls or barks are a plus.

906 ask a riddle

Your youngster's growing vocabulary and verbal skills make hearing and making up riddles a favorite form of humor. Try out this giggle-inducing one:
What's brown and dangerous?
Shark-infested pudding!

 tip *Borrow a "My First Joke Book" from your library and have your little one try out some simple jokes on you.*

907 sew a shirt pillow

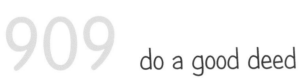

Sew closed the sleeve and bottom hem openings of a beloved but outgrown shirt. Invite your child to stuff it with handfuls of fiberfill from the crafts store. Once she's got it nice and plump, sew up the neck opening to make a comfy pillow she can lounge around on.

908 remember vital info

At five, your child should know his address and phone number as well as his parents' full names. Repetition helps kids learn. Make up a song with the information, or put it to the tune of a favorite song. Sing it over and over until he knows it by heart. Revisit it now and again to make sure he remembers these vital basics.

909 do a good deed

Five-year-olds love helping and pleasing others. Put those altruistic instincts to good use by encouraging your child to bring the neighbors' newspaper up to their door or check a pet's water dish on a hot day. It's fine to praise her for helping others, but ultimately you want her to help just because it's the right thing to do. "May I help?" should become as natural to your child as "Please" and "Thank you."

910 get recycling

Sorting the recycling is easy, and it's never too early to start talking with your little one about the importance of looking after the planet. He will feel good about doing something so practical and at the same time so beneficial to all.

911 write in shaving cream

Put lots of shaving cream on a baking sheet, then invite your child to smooth it out and draw a letter or a number in it. Guess what she's made: "Is it the letter S? The number 5?" She'll love teaching you for a change! (Keep shaving cream away from her mouth and eyes.)

912 paint like a master

Look together at pictures of Michelangelo's Sistine Chapel. Explain that the artist painted the higher sections while lying on his back on some tall scaffolding. Then let your child try it—a bit closer to the ground, of course. Place a drop cloth beneath a low table, tape art paper to the table's underside, and ask him to put on goggles and a smock or an old T-shirt in case of messy drips. Then invite him to recline beneath the table and paint a favorite scene with nontoxic paints. A new perspective can inspire great art!

913 make a bulletin board

Hang a bulletin board at kid height, then demonstrate how to put drawings, party invitations, or photos onto it with magnets. It will remind him of events he's looking forward to, and can also be a way to store mementos of relatives, friends, and vacations.

914 stop and go

The player who is "it" stands at one end of the yard, while the other kids line up at the other. The child who's "it" stands with her back turned to the line of kids and calls out "Green light!" The other kids run toward her, but must stop when she yells "Red light!" Any children she catches still running go back to the start. "It" then repeats the red light–green light cycle until one child reaches and tags her. That child is now "it," and the game starts over again.

915 weave a pot holder

You probably did this craft as a kid yourself. Buy a child's weaving kit with a small square loom and cotton loops. Sit down with your child and teach him how to weave a pot holder. The tradition continues!

916 visit a planetarium

Stargazing with your child on a clear, warm night is one of life's great pleasures. But sometimes it's better to head indoors to a place where you can see the stars and planets in comfort and with greater predictability. Take a trip together to the nearest planetarium and enjoy the sky show.

917 go beyond browsing

Libraries offer great kids' attractions in addition to books to browse. Check out movies, audiobooks, and artwork, for instance. Attend special events like screenings, author readings, and storytimes. See if the library offers incentives for number of books read. Maybe there's even a reading club!

918 study bugs

Get some books from the library or do online research to learn about insects together. The more your child knows about creepy crawlies, the less creepy they are.

 tip *Encourage your child's avid interests—whether bugs, birds, or cars—by visiting the reference librarian.*

919 pop some corn

Popcorn has it all: sound effects, enticing aroma, yummy taste, and near-instant gratification. Make some in the microwave and listen to the pops together. If you have a popper, show your child how to put the kernels in, put on the lid, press "start," and stand back!

920 share sweet sushi

Make sweet "sushi" together. Instead of sticky rice, use treats made from puffed-rice cereal and marshmallow. Tuck gummy fish in the center to take the place of the real thing, and wrap green or blue fruit rolls to stand in for seaweed. Try eating the treats with chopsticks. Your child might be intrigued enough to want to sample real sushi.

921 appreciate music

Most communities offer a variety of free musical events—ranging from symphony rehearsals to outdoor fairs—open to the public. Go together as a family, taking advantage of any opportunities to speak with musicians afterward or to take a look at their instruments up close.

922 celebrate japanese-style

Research Japanese festivals at the library or online and celebrate the ones that appeal to your child. For instance, on Children's Day in Japan, families fly streamers in the shape of fish. Another Japanese celebration with potential kid appeal is the Bean Throwing Festival, when participants toss a few beans for good luck, and eat one bean for each year of their age.

5+ years

923 play with a hula hoop

Playing with a hula hoop is a classic child's game. It's tricky at first, but the more your five-year-old practices, the more skilled she will become at keeping it aloft.

924 try on a new identity

A regular paper plate (not the heavy-duty kind) is the ideal size and weight for making a kid's mask. Punch out two holes, one on each side of the plate. Thread elastic through them, knot the ends, and let your child try the mask on so you can mark the eyeholes. Have him remove the mask and cut out the holes. Let him loose with art supplies and his imagination to become whatever he fancies: wolf, space alien, or clown.

925 hatch a butterfly

Read together about nature's impressive power to transform, then hunt for a caterpillar. Store it in a net-covered, widemouthed jar. Have your child feed it pieces of the plant you found it on until it forms a cocoon. When the butterfly hatches about 10 to 21 days later, release it near where you found the caterpillar.

926 go shopping

Playing pretend grocery store is almost as much fun as going to the real store. It's good practice for learning about money, too.

927 ask probing questions

In "20 Questions," you provide clues to the identity of the person or object you're thinking of in answer to yes-or-no questions, like this:
"Is it a person?"
"Yes."
"Is it a girl?"
"No."
"Is he in the family?"
"Yes."
"Is he tall?"
"Yes."
"Are you thinking of Uncle Ryan?"
"Yes!"

928 design a notepad

Ask your child to make some small, simple line drawings and select his favorite. Then take it to a copy shop to get it reproduced on notepads. Personalized notepads make wonderful presents for teachers, friends, and relatives.

929 a-maze a cat

Join your child in an art project that's fun for the two of you—and for the family cat. Cut the bottoms out of several brown paper grocery bags and tape them together end to end to make a maze for your cat (try to make at least one "tunnel" branching off from the main one). Roll in a small ball to entice your cat to explore.

930 ride a two-wheeler

Depending on your child's height and dexterity, she may be ready to graduate from a tricycle to a bicycle. Straddling the bike, she should be able to put her feet flat on the ground; seated, the balls of her feet should touch the ground. Start with training wheels touching the ground and move them up a little bit every week. Give her lots of encouragement as she gradually improves with each ride. Buy a helmet and make sure your child uses it every time she rides.

931 frolic with frogs

Scientists say that the health and diversity of frogs mirror the health of our planet. Besides, kids love frogs! Look for a frog exhibit at a nearby science museum, zoo, or natural history center to learn about these engaging and fascinating critters. No exhibit nearby? Just visit the nearest pond to check out frogs and their freshwater friends.

932 relocate storytime

On a warm spring or summer evening, surprise your child by moving your nightly storytime outdoors and reading together by flashlight.

933 take a deeper look

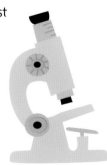

Unleash your child's inner scientist by helping him see the magical structures of simple crystals up close. Set him up in your kitchen "laboratory" with a microscope and staples like table salt, sea salt, or white sugar. Then let him discover how those tiny specks look in detail.

934 kick up a sporty storm

Head outside with your child to get a kick out of playing with balls. Warm up by kicking a soccer ball (or a big rubber ball) back and forth while standing still, then practice passing while running. Once she's a ground-ball pro, show her how to shoot "goals," taking aim at the space between two trees or two park benches. Or keep it light: see who can kick the ball the farthest, the highest, or in the silliest way.

935 get slimy

Whip up some slime with your child! Help him measure a one-to-one ratio of water and cornstarch. Have him mix them (adding a splash of his favorite food coloring) until the goo is smooth—and plenty slimy.

936 play with numbers

Without making it feel like a lesson, engage your child in tasks that involve numerical logic. For instance, show her how to use a measuring tape and she'll likely measure everything in sight. Ask her to help you weigh the cat: have her hold the cat while you weigh them both, then weigh just your child and show her how you subtract that number from the first one to get kitty's weight.

937 jump through hoops

Gather a number of inexpensive hula hoops and lay them on the grass in a range of patterns—say, in pairs, or close together in a long line. Challenge your child to run, hop, or duckwalk along the course and back.

938 map your child's world

Hang a world map on the wall of your child's room. Use colored pins to mark different locations: red for where family members live, green for the countries your relatives came from, blue for places she's heard about or seen in movies or on television. The concept of the map may seem abstract at first, but eventually it will start to make sense: "Hey—Grandpa's from the country we read about in school today!"

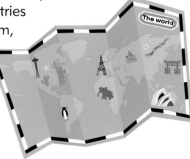

The world

939 look out for letters

Play "alphabet" lotto in the car. Challenge your child to find all the letters of the alphabet on the road signs that you pass during your trip.

940 watch the weather

Teach your child weather-forecasting folklore, like how rain's on the way when the wind blows the leaves so their undersides show. Or how a ring of light around the moon means a cold snap is coming. Watch for these portents together, and keep a weather chart to see if they really do predict the weather accurately.

941 eat an ocean

Mix up a bowl of blue gelatin, and refrigerate to set. Just before it's fully set, insert gummy fish candies in contrasting colors into your gelatin ocean. Float life preserver–shaped candy on top. Ahoy, matey!

942 get set to juggle

Juggling starts with one simple move: tossing an object from one hand to the other in a circular motion. Help your future juggler catch on to the fun by providing him with different items to throw into the air, one at a time, grabbing each item as it falls down. Start with a scarf. Move on to a small beanbag, then to a soft foam ball. Then make it more challenging. Can he do it while slowly walking forward? How about while he's standing on one foot?

943 make rock candy

Have your child put 2 cups (250 grams) of sugar and 1 cup (250 ml) of water into a pot. Bring to a boil (adults only), stirring until the sugar dissolves. Cool slightly, pour into a clean glass jar, and cover with foil. Have your child carefully poke wooden skewers through the foil, not letting them touch the sides or bottom of the jar. After a week or so, sugar crystals will begin to grow on the sticks. Track the crystals' growth. After another week, let her remove the homemade rock candy, study it, and eat it. Science can be tasty!

944 practice writing

A five-year-old learns to write one letter at a time. Encourage him to practice his writing skills by signing every picture he makes.

945 paint faces

Face paint is great fun because it encourages your five-year-old to pretend to be someone or something else—to roar like a tiger, to smile like a clown, to frolic like a puppy, or just be the rainbow kid.

946 go digital

If you're techno-savvy and into all the latest gadgets, your child can be, too. Many libraries let patrons check out electronic books online; if yours is one of them, check out some books your child can listen to on a computer or a portable MP3 player. (Protect her hearing by making sure the volume's not too high.)

5+
years

947 give thanks

Talk about the concept of gratitude together, and then encourage your child to write a thank-you note. Help him with the writing if he needs it—or encourage him to draw a picture that expresses his appreciation for a kind act.

948 make a doll at home

Cut the top flaps, the bottom, and one side from a small corrugated cardboard box, leaving three sides to make an open house for small dolls or plush animals. Use an art knife (adults only) to cut windows and doors, then let your child go to town decorating her toys' new abode with markers or crayons.

949 coil a pot

Start off with a disk of clay, then make a long thin "snake" of clay to coil around it, building higher with every turn. Leave the coil visible or gently press and rub the surface to make it smoother. Have your little one's pot fired at a local kiln.

950 whip up breakfast

Invite your five-year-old to flex his cooking muscles by making breakfast (with lots of adult supervision, of course). To make French toast, mix up eggs, milk, and a little vanilla, then dip in bread slices. Or he could toast bread and top it with butter and jam.

951 label treasures

Buy some polymer clay at a crafts store. Help your child shape some into a small disc, poke a hole in the top with a drinking straw, and press in raw alphabet noodles to spell out the name of a beloved plush animal. Remove the noodles and bake according to the directions on the clay. Make tags for all her favorite friends, and attach them with cord or ribbon.

952 share childhood secrets

Kids love hearing stories from your childhood (especially about times you got into trouble). So share some of your memories—and don't be surprised if your child asks, "Tell me again about the time you and Aunt Susan broke the clock."

953 see fish fly

With your help, have your five-year-old cut out several identical fish shapes, then color and decorate them. Staple two of them together, leaving one side open until he's stuffed it with crumpled newspaper. Make lots of them, and then hang a school of fish from the ceiling.

954 rub different textures

Teach your little one to make rubbings by laying thin paper over three-dimensional surfaces and rubbing them with a peeled crayon or an art pastel. Start with coins or keys, and soon she'll see intriguing rubbing possibilities everywhere: a stone wall, tree bark, a bamboo mat. Make it a game by having her do a few rubbings; then you guess where they came from.

955 stitch a mail pouch

Fold a thin sheet of craft foam in half, punch holes along the sides, and help your child use ribbon to stitch it into a pouch. Hang it up so you have a mail pouch for leaving each other notes or special treats.

956 befriend a grasshopper

Teach your child how to catch a grasshopper (gently). Study the bug quickly before it hops away, or keep it in your bug house (made from a round oatmeal container, with a window cut out and screened with netting) for a little while. Give it some grass to eat. Look at its tiny face and see if you can spot the little holes along its side that it breathes through. What an amazing creature!

957 serve up a slush

Help your child make some slurpy slush—and learn about salty science. Fill a large zip-top bag halfway with ice and a cup of salt, then fill a smaller bag with juice. Put the small bag, zipped, into the big one, and then zip it shut. Wait about 15 minutes for the salt and ice solution to make the juice freeze, shaking the bag often. Then hand her the little bag and a spoon—yum!

958 create a puzzle

Lay eight wooden craft sticks side by side with no gaps, and have your child use nontoxic glue to carefully attach a picture to the sticks. When the glue dries, separate the sticks using an art knife (an adult job). Mix them up and invite him to reassemble the puzzle.

5+
years

959 decorate a pumpkin

Although carving a jack-o'-lantern is an adult job, your child can decorate a pumpkin with simple materials. Help her use nontoxic glue to attach leaves for hair, a carrot tip for a witchy nose, marshmallows for eyes, or rows of corn for a gap-toothed smile. Then have her add finishing touches with nontoxic markers. Spooky!

960 experiment with invisibility

Give your child a cotton swab, some lemon juice, and a white piece of paper, and invite him to dip the swab in the juice to write a secret message or draw a special picture for you. When the paper is dry, show him how to reveal the secret by running a warm iron over the paper (adults only).

961 design finger puppets

Cut the fingers from an old knit glove and invite your child to use nontoxic markers and glue to decorate each of the fingers with ears, tails, faces, dragon scales, and other features made out of materials such as felt, yarn, sequins, and buttons. Then have a puppet show. Afterward, store the puppets in a bag—they're a perfect take-along diversion for a long car ride.

962 bake "ice cream" cakes

Stand flat-bottomed ice cream cones in a muffin pan and help your little baker fill them two-thirds full with cake batter in her favorite flavor. Bake according to your recipe or the mix instructions. Let cool, then help her frost the "cones" and add sprinkles.

963 make your own lotto

Help your child photograph landmarks in your town (such as statues, the fire station, and the middle school where he'll go in a few years). Glue the photos to a piece of white cardboard to make a lotto board, and laminate it so it's reusable. Ask him to put a check mark next to the picture of the landmarks he spots when you're driving or walking through town.

964 fold up art

Together look at a book about origami for kids, then help your child try her hand at making some simple forms. Buy squares of colored origami paper at a crafts store or give her gift wrap, printed paper bags, or even plain printer or notebook paper to cut with safety scissors.

 tip *Folding paper and using age-appropriate scissors improve your five-year-old's fine motor skills.*

965 get the point

Look together at pointillist paintings—that is, those in which the images are made up of tiny dots. (Georges-Pierre Seurat is one of the most famous pointillists.) Once you've studied the style, help your child use nontoxic markers to make a picture using the same technique.

966 squeeze in rhyme time

Five-year-olds are surprisingly adept with rhymes. Encourage that skill by giving your child some books on rhyming and asking him to try finishing a few rhymes himself. Make things even more challenging by asking targeted questions like "What rhymes with *big* and begins with a *P?*"

967 sculpt ice

Cool off on a hot day by using blunt kitchen tools such as spoons to chip and carve away together at blocks of ice you've made by freezing water in clean milk cartons.

968 act it out

A scaled-down version of charades is something your child will relish. Take turns acting out the tasks that go on in her everyday world—such as combing hair, brushing teeth, or driving a car—and then try to guess what the other person is doing. Move on to imitate an animal for each other to identify: leap like a frog, gallop like a horse, or swim like a fish. If she's loving it, take the game a step further and act like her favorite storybook characters. Can she tell that you're skipping down a path with a basket for Grandma, like Little Red Riding Hood? Can you spot her monkeying around like Curious George?

969 teach new tricks

Your child will have a great time teaching the family dog some new moves by rewarding her behaviors as she gets closer and closer to what he wants her to do. For "shake," for instance, have him first reward the dog with a small treat and a "Good dog!" just for sitting down. Then he can take her paw and shake it, saying "Shake!" and giving praise and a treat. Eventually just saying "Shake!" should make the dog raise her paw. With lots of praise and the occasional treat, she'll quickly have the trick down pat.

970 name that animal

5+ years

Hone your child's logical thinking skills and knowledge of nature with an animal guessing game. Give him a new clue after each incorrect guess. The game might go something like this:
"I'm thinking of an animal that lives in Africa."
"Is it a zebra?"
"No. It has spots, not stripes."
"A hyena?"
"No. It's a big cat."
"It's a leopard!"
"Right, it's a leopard!"

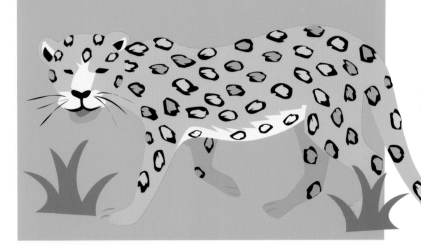

971 listen to simon

Teach your child to play "Simon Says" with a group of friends. Have all the children face the one who is "it," or Simon. That child then dictates a simple activity for the others to do, such as hopping on one foot. The twist is that the activity should be performed only if Simon begins by saying "Simon says." Children who follow instructions that don't start off with those words sit down and wait for the next round. The last child standing becomes the new Simon.

972 color cats

Cut out cat shapes from colored construction paper and lay them in a shallow box. Have your child dip a large marble in colored paint and roll it over the paper cats, using different marbles for each color. When the paint dries, she can use nontoxic markers to add eyes, a nose, a mouth, and whiskers to each one.

973 fashion paper beads

Cut rectangles 3 inches (7.5 cm) long and of various widths from magazine pages or gift wrap. Have your child roll the paper around a pencil and glue it closed with nontoxic glue. Slide off when the glue is dry. String a few of the paper "beads" to make a necklace.

974 write a book

If your five-year-old sees other family members writing (letters, reports, homework), it will seem natural for him to write, too. A blank journal is wonderful for practicing writing the alphabet, doodling, and maybe writing simple sentences. Anytime he's looking for something to do, he can always add to his journal.

975 bake calzone

Cook Italian using a tube of refrigerated roll dough, a jar of pizza sauce, and a little shredded mozzarella. Have her roll the dough into small circles, add a smear of sauce, and finish with a sprinkle of cheese. Help her fold it in half and crimp the edges, then bake the mini calzone (adult job) according to the dough directions.

976 play a dance game

Turn on some peppy music and invite your little dancer to kick up his heels. Sway along, but stay close to the stereo so you can press pause at an unexpected moment and shout, "Freeze!" That's his clue to halt, holding his body still as if "frozen." Turn the music back on and let him continue his footloose antics.

977 plant a terrarium

A large jar can become a great indoor garden. Show your child how to layer small pebbles with potting soil and plant fern and ivy cuttings or succulent seedlings. Have her finish the terrarium with a few decorative stones. Put her in charge of watering and plant care.

978 make a banana octopus

Help your child make an eight-legged friend out of a banana. Have him wash an unpeeled banana, then help him cut eight slits in the bottom of the peel with kitchen shears. Show him how to pull the peel halfway back to lengthen the "tentacles," then help him cut off the exposed fruit with a butter knife for a snack. Have him stand the rest of the banana up and spread the tentacles around its base. Add raisins for eyes.

979 expand chore duties

Kids this age get immense satisfaction from helping out, so put your child to work. Look for chores that are fairly easy, but stretch her logical and mathematical thinking. You might ask her to put the silverware away for you, sorting each piece into the right slot.

980 frame a picture

Have your child use nontoxic paints to make a picture on cardboard, leaving some space around the edges. Then have him use nontoxic glue to attach tiles, shells, buttons, beads, or other treasures around the picture to frame it.

981 see what's in the sea

Take a small, two-handled drift net or mesh bag to the beach, lake, or pond and see what you and your child can scoop up together. (Be sure to supervise water play, and have her put any living creatures you catch back in the water quickly.)

982 find time for a rhyme

Kids love rhythm and silly words, especially when they tell a story. Dig through your (or the library's) bookshelves and find some classic lines of poetry to read and enjoy together. Great poems for children this age include Edward Lear's "The Owl and the Pussycat" and Lewis Carroll's masterpiece of nonsense, "Jabberwocky."

983 assemble a cookie kit

For a gift, have your child layer the makings for cookies in a widemouthed jar, adding each dry ingredient, such as chocolate chips, one by one. Mix the flour with any salt, baking soda, or baking powder before adding. Ask your child to draw a picture of the cookie on a recipe card and attach (recipients add the wet ingredients).

984 play a game of chess

If your five-year-old sees you playing chess, chances are he will be fascinated to learn, too. Start by gently introducing your child to the basics of moving pawns around the board, and you'll be amazed how quickly he picks up the rules of engagement.

985 read a chapter book

Your child will still love her picture books for a long time, but this is a good stage to introduce simple chapter books. She can sit beside you or in your lap and follow along as you read out loud. At bedtime, snuggle with her in bed and read a short chapter aloud, showing her the pictures and pointing out simple, often-repeated words as you go along.

tip *Using cushions and blankets, make a cozy, well-lit corner where your child can read and daydream.*

986 pen a comic strip

Draw or print a series of large boxes on plain paper and show your child how to make his own comic strips. He can start by using the boxes you made and adding some simple characters like thumbprint people or stick figures to tell a joke. Soon he'll be coming up with his own stories.

987 celebrate butterflies

Invite your child to follow a butterfly (from a few feet away, so she doesn't frighten it) as it makes its rounds. Talk about what the butterfly is doing. Does it fly close to the ground or up high? What kinds of flowers does it seem to like best? Back at home, your child can honor her new favorite insect with a "butterfly blot." Have her fold a piece of construction paper in half, cut out the curve of butterfly wings, and unfold the paper. Then she can apply nontoxic paint, refold the paper, then unfold it again. Once the paint dries, she'll have a colorful butterfly to hang on the wall.

988 knit a toy snake

Find an old-fashioned knitting spool at a crafts shop and show your child how to lift loops of yarn over the pins to knit a woolly snake. Sew on some button eyes for dramatic effect.

989 cut costs

Enlist your young shopper's help in clipping coupons (lots of straight lines!) from weekend flyers. Explain how coupons help you save money, then go to the store and encourage your child to help find the bargain items.

990 design a family crest

Draw a large shield shape on stiff paper and invite your child to draw lines dividing the shield into three or four sections. Talk about items he could draw in those sections to represent things or activities that your family enjoys. Help him come up with a motto, something your family believes in or says often.

991 do more with dominoes

Dominoes are wonderful toys for five-year-olds. The game itself is simple to play: just follow the basic rules that come with a domino set. Dominoes provide great practice in taking turns, counting groups of objects at a glance, recognizing patterns, and coming up with winning strategies. When the game's over, they're also great fun to build with.

5+
years

5+
years

992 bake shortcakes

Ask your child to help you measure, mix, roll, and cut biscuits (use your favorite recipe). First, roll the dough out until it's ½ inch (1.25 cm) thick and cut out mini shortcakes with a large cookie cutter. Have him brush the tops with a little milk and sprinkle with a little sugar. Bake according to the recipe. When the cakes are cool, help your child split them open with a fork and cover with strawberries and cream.

993 get psyched for school

If your five-year-old's starting kindergarten this year, it's a great idea to prepare her. One way to build her enthusiasm is to set her up with materials like a blackboard and books so she can play school. Take a day trip together to the school she'll be attending, highlighting aspects you know she'll think are fun: the new playground, the big yellow bus she'll be riding, or the classroom where she'll have a chance to do art projects and meet new playmates.

994 picture a shape

Have your child close her eyes, touch a pencil tip to a piece of paper, and draw a geometric shape in one motion, without peeking or raising the pencil. Now you try it, too!

995 outfit your artist

Outfit your young artist with a traveling art kit. Fill a small backpack with a simple sketchbook, a watercolor pad, paintbrushes, colored pencils, a mini watercolor set, an artist's gum eraser, a small water bottle, and a plastic cup. He will have all the makings for a creative expedition to the woods, the shore—or just the backyard.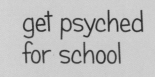

996 hunt for treasure

Take photos of various items around the house: a rocking chair on the porch, a potted plant on the windowsill, Teddy snoozing on your child's bed. Set up a treasure hunt, leaving photo "clues" for her to follow from one place to the next, and include a surprise at the end!

997 fold a usable cup

Working together, fold a piece of paper in half to make a triangle. With the top of the triangle facing away from you, fold the left and right ends inward, so that they meet and overlap along a horizontal line underneath the top of the triangle. Fold the top flaps down in the front and back. Now he can open the cup!

998 watch the skies

Get your child into the sky-watching habit. Study some posters or books about space together. Point out the way the moon goes through its different phases every month. Help her find and track a constellation that's easy to spot, such as Orion or the Big Dipper.

999 climb a tree

For a five-year-old, a tree to climb is as good as a jungle gym. Look for a trunk with low, sturdy branches. Climbing clothes shouldn't have drawstrings, hoods, or anything that might get caught. Set a height limit, and stay nearby.

1000 make chocolaty ghosts

Slowly melt a bag of white chocolate chips in a double boiler (adult job). Pour the melted chocolate into a large zip-top plastic bag and snip a small opening in a bottom corner. Once the bag cools enough to handle it safely, show your child how to squeeze gently to pipe ghostly shapes onto parchment or wax paper. While it's still soft, lay a lollipop stick into the chocolate, and invite your child to add two semisweet chocolate chips for eyes. When they're cool enough, wrap the sweet spooks individually in plastic wrap and store in a cool place.

5+ years

1001 spot animal antics

Visit a zoo with your child and point out animals that illustrate the idea of camouflage. Do some critters use their markings—say, their stripes—to hide in their habitats? What do other animals use?

index

A

Airplanes, 27, 366, 378, 682, 728
Alertness, 4, 61
"All the Pretty Little Horses," 66
Alphabet, 498, 608, 686, 746,
    758, 828, 904, 939
Animals
    approaching, 844
    caring for, 502, 512, 732,
        759, 806, 866, 969
    creating, 567, 685, 768, 840,
        845, 953, 972, 988
    feeding, 443, 521, 701, 712
    homes of, 428, 675
    imitating, 103, 415, 574,
        775, 968
    log of, 839
    naming, 970
    reading books to, 666
    singing about, 394
    watching, 39, 215, 279, 612,
        623, 689, 725, 726, 1001
Ants, 536, 646
Archaeology, 819
Art
    creating, 263, 350, 445, 446,
        463, 474, 489, 494, 496, 510,
        518, 526, 585, 587, 641, 678,
        681, 685, 706, 722, 729, 734,
        751, 755, 768, 787, 797, 817,
        845, 851, 853, 856, 865, 895,
        912, 965, 967, 972
    displaying, 540
    kit, 995
    prehistoric, 853
    supplies, 635

B

Baby toys, 730
Back, patting, 21

Backpacks, 274
"Backward Day," 670
Badminton, 802
Baking, 535, 580, 624, 715,
    753, 760, 801, 863, 962,
    975, 983, 992
Balance, 72, 166, 255,
    264, 424, 634
Balloons, 286
Balls
    balancing on, 72, 264
    batting, 854
    bouncing, 516
    hiding, 229
    kicking, 410, 857, 934
    playing with, 325, 410
    rolling, 457, 617, 825
    tossing, 160
Bananas, 781, 978
Basketball, 832
Baths, 82, 94, 199, 211,
    284, 285, 412, 637,
    695, 746
Bats, 726
Batting, 854
Beaches, 299, 318, 438,
    571, 707
Beads, 508, 762, 794, 826, 973
Beans, 673, 771
Bed, making, 887
Bedtime, 48, 122, 328,
    357, 371, 413
Bells, 115, 441
Bicycles, 323, 930
Birds, 443, 521, 612,
    689, 701, 712
Birthdays, 864
Biting, 392
Blankets, 14, 149, 186,
    194, 300, 356, 393,
    519, 566, 596, 860
Blinking, 32

Blocks, 195, 351, 459, 547, 565
Blowing, on baby, 28
Boats, 783
Bocce, 825
Body awareness, 95, 99, 198, 600
Body language, 4, 407
Body parts, naming, 15, 44, 157,
    205, 319, 375
Bolstering, 108
Book bags, 470
Bookmarks, 794
Books
    activity, 181
    choosing, 461, 756, 790, 795
    creating, 214, 583, 621, 815,
        897, 974
    electronic, 946
    inspiration from, 548, 889
    page turners for, 342
    reading, 33, 218, 304, 321, 402,
        422, 423, 506, 666, 700, 740,
        795, 883, 985
    recording, 296
    storing, 399
    swapping, 886
Bookstores, 383
Bouncing, 123, 166, 516
Bowling, 617
Boxes, 196, 261, 266, 428, 473,
    568, 602, 782, 948
Bracelets, 74
Breakfast, 757, 950
Brooms, 331, 434, 822
Bubbles, 101, 164, 173, 272,
    446, 582, 763, 799
"Bug-a-Boo's Got Feet," 205
Bugs, 379, 448, 657, 667, 684,
    703, 877, 918, 956
Building toys, 572, 709
Bulletin boards, 913
"Bunny" salad, 638
Buses, 455

Butter, 663
Butterflies, 667, 925, 987

C

Cakes, 580, 962
Calculators, 786
Calendars, 820
Calzone, 975
Camping, 770
Candy, 943, 1000
Card games, 808, 892
Car rides, 41, 43, 63, 337, 426,
    610, 615, 812, 884, 939, 963
Carrying, 19, 104, 114, 137
Cars, toy, 561, 572, 665, 782
Car washes, 662
Caterpillars, 667, 925
Catnip, 813
Cause and effect, 136, 239, 246
Chalk, 626, 769
Changes, making, 58, 542
Charades, 968
Charity, 850, 909
Chasing games, 100, 282
Checkers, 867
Cheek game, 281
Chess, 984
Children, watching and playing
    with other, 111, 294, 466, 821
Chores, 110, 349, 364, 437, 444,
    511, 593, 822, 979
Clapping, 244, 297, 784
Clay, 552, 739, 801, 949, 951
Climbing, 260, 315, 541, 879, 999
"The Clock Stands Still," 421
Clothing, 10, 78, 442, 484, 497,
    575, 640, 670, 742, 855, 907
Clovers, four-leaf, 807
Coaching, 650
Collages, 685, 707, 774, 895
Collections, 652, 811

Colors, 309, 312, 559, 579, 589,
    674, 731, 798
"Come to the Window," 122
Comforting, 34, 373, 429, 435,
    495, 588, 596
Comic strips, 986
Commands, following, 439, 553
Computers, 671
Contests, 871
Cookies, 535, 624, 760, 983
Cooking, 367, 427, 471, 563, 648,
    781, 950, 1000
Coughing, 132
Counting, 118, 387, 733, 861
Coupons, 989
Crafts show, 859
Crawling, 144, 153, 201, 242
Crayons, 389, 474, 579, 595,
    615, 831
Crowns, 368
Cruising, 308, 381
Crying, 69
Crystals, 933, 943
Cupcakes, 645
Cups, 306, 425, 997
Cushions, 395, 460
Cycling exercise, 13

D

Dancing, 20, 96, 148, 976
Dandelions, 607
Daydreaming, 31
Diaper changes, 23
Dinosaurs, 493, 699
Distractions, 88, 140, 193, 224,
    314, 389, 480
Dolls, 376, 517, 609, 702, 888, 948
Dominoes, 724, 991
Doorbells, 177
Drawing, 263, 474, 585, 734, 797,
    817, 965, 994

Dress-up, playing, 505, 640
Dropping games, 188, 246,
    358, 385
Duck feet, 676

E

Emergency skills, 862, 869,
    902, 908
Encouragement, 287, 555, 650
Environment, caring for,
    780, 848, 910
Exercise, 90, 190
Exploration, 344, 411, 642, 805
Eye contact, 2, 83
Eye-foot coordination, 136
Eye-hand coordination, 94, 183,
    246, 272, 277, 364, 644

F

Face paint, 945
Faces, 3, 25, 37, 68
Fairies, 592, 842
Family
    crest, 990
    interaction, 62
    newsletter, 894
    tree, 791
Fans, 843
"The Farmer's Horse," 161
Farmers' markets, 551
Farms, 428, 599, 623, 721, 725
Favorites, playing, 488
Fears, 435, 465, 495
Feelings, 476, 519
Feet, 52, 134, 170, 223, 295,
    406, 464, 600, 676
Felt, 556, 898
Finger painting, 339, 496
Fingerplays, 55, 150, 165, 336,
    345, 418, 467, 482

Fingerprints, 463, 587, 849
Fingers, 38, 416, 467, 522
Fireflies, 877
Fire station, 882
First-aid kit, 800
Fish, 39, 740, 796, 837, 953
"Five Little Monkeys," 627
Flashlights, 54, 139, 486,
    566, 661, 872, 932
Floor gym, 81
Flowers, 40, 562, 688, 788, 803
Flying games, 27, 253, 366
Food, playing with, 332, 440, 496
Footprints, 75, 405, 778, 842
Frames, 744, 814, 980
Freezing, 514, 692, 737
"Frère Jacques," 116
Friendships, 690, 821
Frogs, 931

G

Garden centers, 487
Gardens, 151, 458, 632, 667,
    688, 704, 771, 833, 876, 977
Ghosts, chocolate, 1000
Glass doors, 450
"Go Fish," 808
Good-bye, 278, 361
Graham crackers, 350
Granola, 715
Grasshoppers, 956
Greetings, 70, 210
Growth charts, 754

H

Hair, 347, 412
Hammers, 288, 404, 434
Hammocks, 47, 384
Hands, 38, 65, 74, 97, 237, 578
Hardware stores, 382

Harmonicas, 558
Hats, 204, 346
Head lifts, 79
"Head, Shoulders, Knees, and Toes,"
    319
Hearing, sense of, 391
Heartbeats, 1
Hearts, 865
Herbs, 704
"Here Is a Beehive," 345
"Hickory Dickory Dock," 387
Hiding games, 182, 185, 203,
    216, 219, 229, 240, 247,
    259, 270, 306, 311, 396,
    452, 490, 515, 527, 639
Hiking, 792
Hopping, 236, 264, 727
Hospital, for toys, 517
"How Do You Like to Go Up in a
    Swing," 102
Hugs, 76, 435
Hula hoops, 923
Humor, 200, 249, 513,
    588, 741, 906

I

Ice, 106, 967
Ice cream cone cakes, 962
"I Knew a Man Called Michael
    Finnegan," 660
"I'm a Little Walker," 330
Imitating, 11, 37, 80, 147, 206,
    288, 293, 341, 434, 437
"In a Cabin in the Woods," 482
Independence, 453
Initials, 608, 613
Ink, invisible, 960
Inkblots, 767
"Intery, Mintery, Cattery Corn," 483
"I Spy," 581, 597
"It's Raining, It's Pouring," 398

"The Itsy-Bitsy Spider," 55
"I Woke Up This Morning," 165

J

Jack-in-the-box, 280
Jack-o'-lanterns, 959
Jams, 677
Japanese festivals, 922
Jars, 227, 313, 329,
    344, 977
Jellies, 427
Jewelry, 562, 664, 739,
    810, 826, 898, 973
Jogging, 190
"John Jacob Jingleheimer
    Schmidt," 84
Journals, 75
Juggling, 241, 942
Jumping, 174, 537
Jump ropes, 893

K

Kazoos, 451, 901
Kicking, 136, 857
Kisses, 57, 134, 180, 206,
    217, 248, 258, 456
Kites, 187
Knee rides, 64, 161, 163, 228,
    359, 408, 483, 627
Knees, bending, 222
Knitting, 988

L

Ladybugs, 379, 764
Languages, foreign, 116, 733, 864
Lanterns, 472
Laughing, 129, 249, 513, 588
Laundry, 349, 436, 437, 549, 742
Laundry baskets, 252

Leaves, 171, 363, 611, 816, 899
Lemonade, 830
Libraries, 399, 462, 829, 917, 946
License plates, 884
Lights, 239
"Little Ducky Duddle," 365
"The Little Train Goes up the Track," 336
Logical thinking, 619, 719, 970
Lullabies, 380
Lunch bags, 716

m

Mad scientist, playing, 591
Magazines, 310, 538
Magic carpet, 533
Magnets, 305, 693
Magnifying glass, 520, 816
Mail, 530
Mail pouch, 955
Maps, 649, 938
Maracas, 507
Marbles, 836
Masks, 603, 924
Massages, 36, 52, 77, 295, 307, 388
Matching games, 547, 569, 604, 742
Math skills, 714, 733, 786, 861, 870, 936
Mealtime, 109, 198, 208, 231, 237, 269, 374, 550, 560, 638, 766, 950
Memories, sharing, 447, 952
Memory games, 447
Messes, 409, 618, 798
Microscopes, 933
Milk, 494, 852
Mirrors, 3, 179, 204, 362, 500, 734

Mistakes, 564
Mobiles, 31, 46, 141
Monkey bread, 863
"Monkey See, Monkey Do," 341
Moose, 845
Mosaics, 673
Mouth, putting things in, 86, 142
Movies, 643
"Mr. Knickerbocker," 189
Muffin pans, 251
Museums, 327, 793
Music
  box, 93
  dancing to, 20, 148, 976
  listening to, 16, 127, 352, 417, 554, 616, 827, 921
  making, 124, 230, 451, 454, 491, 507, 524, 558, 577, 644, 901
  shops, 789

N

Nachos, 765
Nakedness, 99, 198, 442
Names, 35, 155, 485, 711, 758
Necklaces, 562, 664, 739, 810, 826, 898, 973
Nets, 981
Nighttime activities, 570, 683, 770, 877, 932
"No," saying, 504
Notepads, 928
Numbers, 659, 828, 861, 936
Nut butter, 891

O

Oatmeal, 757
Object permanence, 240, 259, 261, 396
Obstacle courses, 242, 326, 381, 710, 871, 874, 937

Ocean scenes, 868, 941
Octopus, 567, 978
"Oh, Baby's on My Knee," 64
"Oh Where, Oh Where," 194
"Old MacDonald," 200, 394
"One Potato, Two Potato," 658
"One, Two, Three Big Stars," 118
Oobleck, 651
Opposites, 620
Origami, 647, 964
Outings, 63, 87

P

Painting, 254, 339, 405, 432, 445, 510, 518, 535, 589, 735, 751, 912, 945
Pancakes, 367, 747
Paper dolls, 888
Paperweights, 881
Parachutes, 133
Parfaits, 601
Party poppers, 834
Patience, 71
Patterns, following, 297, 508, 547
Peekaboo, 51, 138, 219, 259, 396
Pennies, cleaning, 606
Perspective, changing, 73, 104, 213
Pets, 486, 502, 512, 666, 732, 806, 813, 814, 866, 929, 969
Phones, 225, 275, 841, 862
Photos, 184, 481, 583, 717, 723, 838, 888, 902, 963
Physical contact, 19, 21, 29, 34, 76
Picking-up games, 397, 534
Picnics, 544
Piggy banks, 885
Pillows, 85, 907
Pineapples, 745
Pinwheels, 30
Pipe cleaners, 729

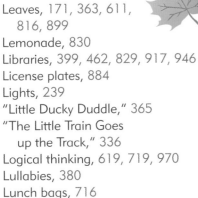

Pizzas, 471, 648, 653
Place settings, 598
Planetariums, 916
Plants, 317, 531, 629, 688, 704, 745, 771, 813, 824, 833, 977
Play dates, 294, 466, 875
Playgrounds, 501, 656, 879
Plays, 818
"Please," 360
Plush animals, 371, 515, 517, 549, 568
Poetry, 878, 982
Pony rides, 809
Popcorn, 165, 919
Postcards, 530, 751
Potato prints, 622
Pot holders, 915
Pots, 343, 949
Pouring, 94, 285, 335, 852
Praise, 287
Pretzels, 713, 753
Primitive art, 853
Pumpkins, 599, 959
Puppets, 97, 113, 216, 258, 334, 477, 522, 636, 669, 687, 905, 961
Push and pull game, 340
Push toys, 256, 400
Pussy willows, 708
Puzzles, 292, 390, 543, 655, 744, 958

Q

Questions, 128, 447, 630, 719, 927
Quiet time, 31, 162, 212, 393, 417, 480, 738
Quilts, 691, 772

R

Rainbows, 175, 463
Rain sticks, 178, 590

Rainy days, 135, 167, 365, 395, 398, 545
"Raspberries," blowing, 338
Rattles, 42, 197, 290
Reaching, 56, 130, 144, 241, 298, 337
Recycling, 910
"Red and Orange," 312
"Red Light, Green Light," 914
Restaurants, 88, 586
Rhyming, 122, 528, 680, 741, 966, 982
Rhythm, 297, 423
Ribbons, 45
Riddles, 906
"Ride a Cockhorse," 163
"Ring-Around-the-Rosy," 492
Rings, stacking, 277
Rock candy, 943
Rocking, 59, 291
Rocks, 518, 706, 811
Rolling over, 98
Room decorations, 856
"Round and Round the Baby's Feet," 15
"Round and Round the Garden," 154,
Routines, 48, 355, 413, 717
"Row, Row, Row Your Boat," 118, 220, 475
Rubbings, 954

S

Safety drills, 902
Sand play, 318, 414, 431, 438, 698, 787
Sandwiches, 543, 557
Scarves, 183, 401
Scavenger hunts, 538, 777
School, 993
Scissors, 594, 697
Scrapbooks, 804, 899

Seeds, 833, 851
Self-portraits, 797
Separation anxiety, 270, 278, 499
Shadows, 54, 578, 903
Shapes, 262, 503, 774, 994
Sharing, 529, 576
Shells, 707, 739, 810
Shirts, 497, 855, 907
"Shoe a Little Horse," 159
Shoelaces, 525, 858
Shoes, 322, 424, 896
Shopping, 140, 193, 604, 694, 926, 989
Shopping carts, 400
Shortcakes, 992
Sign language, 234
Silhouettes, 903
"Simon Says," 320, 971
"Sippity Sup," 269
Sitting, 85, 146
Sit-ups, 60
"Slap Jack," 892
Slides, 268
Slime, 935
Slush, 957
Smell, sense of, 40, 267, 509
Smiling, 8, 70
Smoothies, 539
S'mores, 835
Snacks, 536, 546, 580, 608, 614, 664, 713, 766
Sneezing, 120
Snow, 489, 750
Snowflakes, paper, 900
Soccer, 934
Social skills, 360, 909, 947
Socks, 113, 223, 240, 436, 477, 668
Softball, 854
Somersaults, 880
Songs, sharing, 121, 370, 735
Sorting, 386, 436, 532

Sounds
    hearing, 26
    locating, 126, 182
    making, 9, 24, 92, 105, 119, 140,
        176, 177, 197, 235, 245, 273,
        343, 354, 451, 479, 491
    repeating, 152
Speech balloons, 873
Spiders, 55, 775
Sponges, 199, 526, 752
Spoons, 88, 176, 208, 209, 245,
    354, 524
Sports, 802, 832, 854, 934
Stacking, 277, 302, 303,
    351, 425, 459
Standing, 168
Stairs, 260, 541
Stamps, 773
Stars, 357, 570, 661,
    916, 998
Stickers, 357, 450
Strangers, 403, 420
Stretching, 18, 736
Sunglasses, 847
Surprises, 743
Sushi, 920
Swimming, 283, 776, 846
Swinging, 47, 102, 125, 158,
    210, 749
Syllables, 784

T

Tags, 951
Talking
    to child, 12, 33, 107, 128,
        156, 192, 243, 301, 447
    first words, 333
    practicing, 91
    recording, 226, 296
    volume of, 145
Tambourines, 454

Taste, sense of, 631, 779
Tea
    parties, 316, 419
    sun, 761
Teeth, 238, 679
Telephones, 225, 275, 841, 862
Terrariums, 977
Textures, 7, 112, 303, 430, 954
"Thank you," 232, 360, 947
"This Is the Way the Farmer Rides,"
    359
"This Is the Way We Brush Our
    Teeth," 238
"This Little Piggy," 50, 372
Throwing games, 385, 401, 478
Tickling, 22, 143, 154, 159, 205
"Tick Tock, Tick Tock," 158
Tic-tac-toe, 671, 785
Time, 633, 820
Tongue twisters, 625
Touch, sense of, 86, 329
Toy inventory, 468
Toys, offering, 43, 49, 119, 221,
    386, 426
Trail mix, 720
Trains, 568, 584
Transitional objects, 186
Transitions, 875
Treasure boxes, 823
Treasure hunt, 996
Trees, 5, 824, 999
Tricycles, 628, 672
"Trot, Little Pony," 408
Tug-of-war, 169, 718
Tunnels, 202
"20 Questions," 639, 927
"Two Little Blackbirds Sitting on a
    Hill," 467

U, V

Umbrellas, 250

Up and down, 89
Variety, encouraging, 605, 694, 748
Videotaping, 523
Vines, 629
Vision
    stimulating, 17, 46, 49, 53, 67,
        83, 141
    testing, 391
Visual tracking, 25, 139, 172, 306

W

Wagons, 276, 511
Walking, 6, 265, 271, 330,
    469, 545
"Wash the Dishes," 418
Water play, 94, 199, 207, 211,
    233, 246, 254, 283, 284,
    353, 369, 377, 432, 433,
    437, 561, 654, 846
"Water, Water Everywhere," 135
Waving, 278, 361
Weather, 705, 940
Wheelbarrow game, 257
"Where Is Baby?" 138
"Where Is Thumbkin?" 416
Whistling, 92
Wind chimes, 26
Work space, 890
Worms, 696
Wrapping paper, 289, 324
Writing, 573, 872, 911, 944, 974

X, Y, Z

Xylophones, 644
"Yankee Doodle," 150
Yarn, 411, 722
Yoga, 117, 348, 736
Zoos, 279, 394, 725, 1001

GYMBOReE PLAY&MUSIC®

Produced by Weldon Owen Inc., 814 Montgomery Street, San Francisco, California 94133,
in collaboration with the Gymboree Play Programs, 500 Howard Street, San Francisco, California 94105.

CONSULTING EDITORS

Dr. Roni Cohen Leiderman has a Ph.D. in developmental psychology and specializes in early childhood development, curriculum design, positive discipline, parenting, and play. For more than 25 years, she has worked with children, families, and professionals at the Mailman Segal Institute for Early Childhood Studies at Nova Southeastern University.

Dr. Wendy Masi is a developmental psychologist specializing in early childhood. She has both designed and implemented programs for early childhood professionals, preschools, and families with young children for more than 25 years at the Mailman Segal Institute for Early Childhood Studies at Nova Southeastern University.

AUTHORS

Susan Elisabeth Davis is the author of activities 1–334. She wrote Gymboree's *365 Activities You and Your Baby Will Love* and *Baby Play*; she coauthored *Toddler Play*.

Nancy Wilson Hall is the author of activities 335–1001. She wrote Gymboree's *365 Activities You and Your Toddler Will Love* and *365 Activities You and Your Child Will Love*.

ILLUSTRATOR

Christine Coirault, a children's book illustrator based in London, is the illustrator of *How Do I Say That?* and the author of *The Little Book of Good Manners*.

PHOTOGRAPHERS

Aimée Herring: photos for activities 18 and 491

Aaron Locke: photos for front cover (bottom left); chapter introductions for 0+, 3+, 6+, and 9+ months; and activities 46, 73, 129, 156, 241, 269, 297, and 325

Tosca Radigonda: photos for front cover (top left and right); chapter introductions for 12+, 18+, 24+, and 30+ months; and activities 101, 351, 381, 409, 435, 465, 519, 549, 576, 605, and 659

John Robbins: photos for chapter introductions for ages 3+, 4+, and 5+ years; and activities 724, 833, and 945

Crystal Young: photos for activities 213 and 633

Gymboree Play & Music
Chief Executive Officer Matthew McCauley
VP, Gymboree Play & Music Jill Johnston
Merchandise Manager Dawn Sagorski
Senior Program Developer Helene Silver Freda

Key Porter Books Limited
Six Adelaide Street East, Tenth Floor
Toronto, Ontario Canada M5C 1H6
www.keyporter.com

Weldon Owen Group
Chief Executive Officer John Owen
Chief Financial Officer Simon Fraser

Weldon Owen Inc.
Chief Executive Officer, President Terry Newell
Senior VP, International Sales Stuart Laurence
VP, Sales & Marketing Amy Kaneko

VP, Creative Director Gaye Allen
Designers Renée Myers and Emma Forge

VP, Publisher Roger Shaw
Executive Editor Elizabeth Dougherty
Project Editors Karen Zuercher and Corinne Roberts
Editorial Assistant Sarah Gurman

Production Director Chris Hemesath
Production Manager Michelle Duggan
Color Manager Teri Bell

Library and Archives Canada Cataloguing in Publication

Hall, Nancy.
   Play & learn: 1,001 fun activities for your baby and child/Nancy Hall & Susan Elisabeth Davis; Roni Cohen Leiderman & Wendy Masi, consulting editors; Christine Coirault, illustrator.

ISBN 978-1-55470-033-2

   1. Preschool children—Recreation.
2. Play. 3. Child development. 4. Child rearing. I. Davis, Susan E., 1961-
II. Leiderman, Roni III. Masi, Wendy S.
IV. Coirault, Christine V. Title. VI. Title: Play and learn.

HQ782.H34 2008   649'.5   C2007-904856-0

about gymboree

A pioneer in promoting the educational benefits of play, Gymboree has a simple philosophy: fun-filled play is the ideal way to give kids a great start in life. Based on established principles of early childhood education and led by trained teachers, Gymboree Play & Music classes have helped parents and children enjoy together the wonders of play, art, and music since 1976. Today, Gymboree offers interactive parent-child programs in more than 30 countries.

a special note on safety

When doing the activities described in this book with your child, please take every precaution to ensure that your child is safe at all times. To reduce the risk of injury, do not leave your child unattended, even for a brief moment, during any of the activities in this book; be particularly cautious when participating in the activities involving water because of the risk of drowning; ensure that your child does not place in his or her mouth any small objects (even those depicted in the photographs and illustrations), as some may pose a choking hazard and could be fatal if ingested; remove crib mobiles once your baby can push up onto hands and knees; and make sure that writing and crafts materials are nontoxic and have been approved for use by children your child's age.

This book suggests guidelines on the age appropriateness of the activities; however, please assess the suitability of any activity for your child before attempting it. While we have made every effort to ensure that the information is accurate and reliable, and that the activities are safe and workable with adult supervision, we disclaim all liability for any unintended, unforeseen, or improper application of the recommendations and suggestions featured in this book.